# NELSON MANDELA

# NELSON MANDELA

·

*Elleke Boehmer*

A BRIEF
INSIGHT

STERLING

New York / London
**www.sterlingpublishing.com**

STERLING and the distinctive Sterling logo are registered trademarks of
Sterling Publishing Co., Inc.


Library of Congress Cataloging-in-Publication Data

Boehmer, Elleke, 1961-
 Nelson Mandela : a very short introduction / Elleke Boehmer.
    p. cm. -- (Brief insights)
 Includes bibliographical references and index.
 ISBN 978-1-4027-6889-7 (alk. paper)
1. Mandela, Nelson, 1918- 2. Presidents--South Africa--Biography. 3. Political prisoners--South
Africa--Biography. 4. South Africa--Politics and government--20th century. I. Title.
 DT1949.M35B64 2009
 968.06'5092--dc22
 [B]

                                                                    2009025877


10  9  8  7  6  5  4  3  2  1


Published by Sterling Publishing Co., Inc.
387 Park Avenue South, New York, NY 10016
Published by arrangement with Oxford University Press, Inc.


© 2008 by Elleke Boehmer
Illustrated edition published in 2010 by Sterling Publishing Co., Inc.
Additional text © 2010 Sterling Publishing Co., Inc.


Distributed in Canada by Sterling Publishing
c/o Canadian Manda Group, 165 Dufferin Street
Toronto, Ontario, Canada M6K 3H6


Book design: The DesignWorks Group


Please see picture credits on page 210 for image copyright information.


Printed in China
All rights reserved


Sterling ISBN 978-1-4027-6889-7


For information about custom editions, special sales, premium and
corporate purchases, please contact Sterling Special Sales
Department at 800-805-5489 or specialsales@sterlingpublishing.com.

**Frontispiece:** This photograph of Nelson Mandela was taken in 1994, during a campaign meeting
in the South African region of KwaZulu-Natal before that year's presidential election. Mandela
became the first president in the country's history to be elected by a fully representative constituency.

*Aan mijn familie*

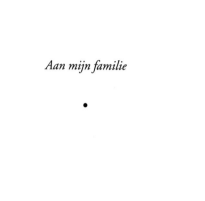

# CONTENTS

•

# ACKNOWLEDGMENTS

•

I HAVE NOTCHED UP A GREAT MANY DEBTS in the course of writing this book. In roughly chronological order warm thanks go to:

Mark Allix, co-navigator through the streets of Johannesburg in the 1980s;

Rob Nixon, whose essay "Mandela, Messianism, and the Media" opened new insights;

Robert Young, whose *Postcolonialism* set an inspiring example;

Stephen Morton and Alex Tickell, conversations with whom about colonial terror helped foster this study;

Achille Mbembe, for thoughts on violence in the postcolony;

Leela Gandhi and Catherine Clarke, for saying that a reflective postcolonial study of Mandela was long overdue;

Ed Larrissy and the School of English, University of Leeds, Simon Glendinning and the European Forum, and Mieke Bal and her ASCA team in Amsterdam, for hosting my papers on Mandela the "postcolonial terrorist" at their conferences in 2005 and 2006;

The journal *Parallax* for publishing the article "Postcolonial Terrorist: The Example of Nelson Mandela" in their special issue 37 on "Agitation" (October–December 2005) that grew out of these papers;

Tim Brennan and Keya Ganguly, fellow guests at the ASCA conference, for their searching and sustaining questions;

Marsha Filion, and Luciana O'Flaherty and James Thompson at Oxford University Press, for their encouragement and help;

Derek Attridge and David Attwell, for moral support and good guidance;

Geerthi Ahilan and her 2004–5 Year 5 group at St Ebbe's C-of-E-aided Primary School, for confronting the question "Who is Nelson Mandela?";

The Department of English at Royal Holloway, University of London, in particular the informal grant workshop group of Bob Eaglestone, Christie Carson, and Jenny Neville; also HoD Robert Hampson, fellow DoGS Ewan Fernie, Anne Varty, my commuting companion, and the irreplaceable Alice Christie—all for much appreciated help and encouragement;

The AHRC Research Leave Award AN/E503543/1 which indispensably facilitated the writing-up period;

The wonderful Royal Holloway Postcolonial Research Group, for engaging with my still-unformed ideas about Mandela, in particular Helen Gilbert (for her thoughts on postcolonial performing bodies), David Lambert (for his remarkable analytic insights), and Nicole King (for her deep knowledge of African-American writing and politics);

Danielle Battigelli and James Rogers, for their enthusiasm and the logo-bearing apron;

Jo McDonagh, for Derrida's *Specters* and strong cups of tea;

Susheila Nasta, my co-editor on the *Wasafiri* special "Cultures of Terror" issue, for her insightful advice;

Shaun Johnson, CEO of the Mandela Rhodes Foundation, for indulging my speculations concerning the Madiba phenomenon;

The Department of English, University of Stellenbosch, especially Dirk Klopper and Meg Samuelson, for hosting me during a crucial period of research toward this book;

Sarah Nuttall who, rescuing me from a rainy Cape weekend, sat me down at a table spread with art books, vivid insights, and baby toys;

Isabel Hofmeyr, for her historical pointers and inspiration;

Simphiwe Yako and Andre Mohammed, archivists at the Mayibuye Archive, University of the Western Cape, and Carol Archibald of the Historical Papers Section, Cullen Library, University of the Witwatersrand, for their advice and help;

David Medalie, intrepid navigator through the streets of Johannesburg, especially Kort Street, at rush hour, in 2006;

Karina Szczurek and Andre Brink, for their hospitality and helpful points of reference;

The Center of Memory and Dialogue at the Nelson Mandela Foundation, especially Project Manager Verne Harris, for invaluable research support;

Mike Nicol, for invigorating e-mail chats about Madiba hagiography;

Judith Brown, for her thoughts about Gandhi the Victorian gentleman;

Josée Boehmer-Dekker, Ilona Berkhof, and the Thuiszorg team in Den Haag, for their fantastic help during my mother's final year, which was also the final year of this book's making;

Sandra Assersohn, inspired picture researcher;

Alison Donnell, Saul Dubow, and Steven Matthews, for thoughtful readings of the final manuscript at a busy time, and William Beinart for his attuned and measured commentary;

Steven Matthews, again, and Thomas and Sam Matthews Boehmer, for keeping the world turning, and the sun spinning through the sky.

Kind acknowledgment goes to Faber and Faber, Ltd., for permission to quote "Brief Dream" from *Collected Poems* by Samuel Beckett (2007). The poem first appeared in Jacques Derrida and Mustafa Tlili, eds., *For Nelson Mandela* (Seaver Books, 1986).

# ABBREVIATIONS

•

| | |
|---|---|
| AAM | Anti-Apartheid Movement |
| ANC | African National Congress |
| BCM | Black Consciousness Movement |
| MK | Umkhonto we Sizwe ("Spear of the Nation") |
| PAC | Pan-Africanist Congress |
| SACP | South African Communist Party |
| SAIC | South African Indian Congress |
| TRC | Truth and Reconciliation Commission |
| UDF | United Democratic Front |
| ANCYL | African National Congress Youth League |

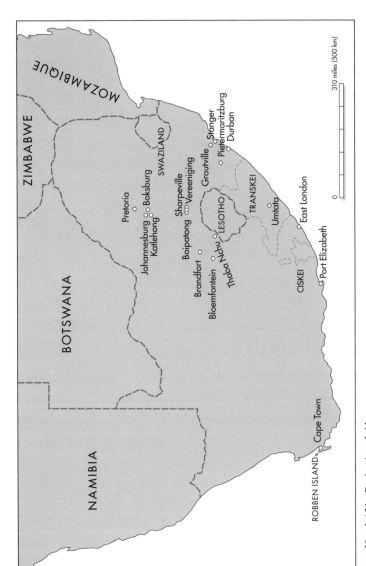

Map of South Africa During Apartheid

# ONE

## Mandela: Story and Symbol

•

HIS GIVEN XHOSA NAME *Rolihlahla* signified he could be a troublemaker. His clan honorific *Madiba* associated him with his aristocratic Thembu lineage. And his European name *Nelson*, his best-known name, given by his primary school teacher, imprinted his life with the name of one of imperial Britain's naval heroes. Between these three nodal points of his names—signifying resistance, social stature, and heroism, respectively—Nelson Rolihlahla Mandela's life has played out in extraordinary, mythmaking ways. His face and his form, his raised-arm salute and walk into freedom, are among the most widely reproduced icons of the twentieth century.

Nelson Mandela—is it possible to say, in a phrase, who or what he is? Yes, he was one of the world's longest-detained political prisoners; during the time of his incarceration easily its most famous. He is a universal symbol of social justice certainly, an exemplary figure connoting nonracialism and

**A few months after his release from prison,** on April 16, 1990, Mandela spoke to the crowd at a celebratory concert in his honor at Wembley Stadium in London.

democracy, a moral giant. Once a man without a face (photographs of political prisoners in South Africa being banned), he became after his 1990 release an internationally recognizable image. For over four decades, while his country was vilified the world over for its policies of state-sanctioned racism, called apartheid, Mandela symbolically and to some extent practically led the movement of resistance to that injustice.

But why should his story be important to us in the world at large today? What do his achievements signify, not only nationally in South Africa but also internationally? How do we justify yet another short introduction covering the events of his long life? To be sure, he is a hero in his own country, whose freedom he worked to win. But how is it that he became a big name worldwide also—a prominent figure in the campaign to raise HIV/AIDS awareness; the 2006 Amnesty International Ambassador of Conscience; a moniker in UK comedy shows (Mark Thomas's *As Used on the Famous Nelson Mandela*)? Why is it his face above all others (including Gandhi's) that is chosen to grace the covers of potted histories of our time? How was it that at the time of the unveiling of his statue in Westminster Square in the summer of 2007, he was hailed as "President of the World" (by analogy with the "People's Princess" Diana)?

In the celebrity culture that marks the new millennium, with its focus on the individual as maker of their destiny, it is often assumed that Mandela was not only the master of his individual fate, but the chief architect of the new South Africa. It is taken as read that he fought a single-handed fight for the rights of black people, and that in his case the theory that Great Men make history is well justified. And yet, as he himself often reminded people, his nation South Africa's liberation struggle was effectively fought for and won while he languished in jail. Already at his 1962 trial he emphasized, "I have been only one in a large army of people."

· · · · ·

"If one wanted an example of an absolutely upright man, that man, that example would be Mandela. If one wanted an example of an unshakably firm, courageous, heroic, calm, intelligent, and capable man, that example and that man would be Mandela. I did not just reach this conclusion after having met him in person. . . . I have thought this for many years. I identify him as one of the most extraordinary symbols of this era."

*Fidel Castro, from "We Will Never Return to the Slave Barracks" (1991)*

· · · · ·

His personal charisma is of course palpable and itself famous. All who have met him remark on the charm, the *Madiba magic*, that radiates from him: a combination of his fame, height, and good looks, his encyclopedic memory for faces, plus an indefinable something else, an attractive Mandela-esque *je ne sais quoi*. Central to his character, writes his admirer the novelist Nadine Gordimer, is "a remove from self-centeredness, the capacity to live for others." His good guidance and charisma represented important sources of inspiration for the making of post-1994 South Africa. Yet it is also true that he did not himself strictly speaking author that new democracy. With Mandela it is manifestly the case that his leadership *alone* cannot explain the historical development in South Africa from apartheid to freedom. Inner radiance alone cannot account for why his icon should bulk large in the world's imagination.

The true picture—the real-life constituents of Madiba magic—is a great deal more complicated than the story of individual specialness suggests. It is based in a quality of character certainly, but this is combined with other key factors which this book addresses, not least his talent as a performer, and career-long proximity to several outstanding colleagues and friends, themselves astute political minds, especially Oliver Tambo, Walter Sisulu, and Ahmed Kathrada. Then there are the ways in which his social makeup impacted on political developments in his country, especially in the 1950s, and how he shaped and reshaped his nationalist stance in response to those developments, while also increasingly reaching for transnational models of resistance, and appealing to an international audience. Throughout, he both referenced and drew upon, yet worked in skillful counterpoint to, his highborn background and its legacies of consensual authority, in order to shape the democratic, collective leadership structures of his organization, the African National Congress (ANC).

· · · · ·

"More than any other living person, Nelson Mandela has come to symbolize all that is hopeful and idealistic in public life."

*Bill Shipsey, Art for Africa founder, on Mandela's 2006*
*Amnesty International Ambassador of Conscience Award*

· · · · ·

A mundane point to make about a memorable man it may be, yet Nelson Mandela is one of those historical figures who, in the mid- to late 1950s, and then in the 1980s and 1990s, was not merely the right man to stand forth at the right time. He was also, importantly, the one who did so with notable political acumen, adaptability, and style, as well as self-consciously and determinedly. At a time when the polarized racial struggle in South Africa justified a sharp turn from till-then effective passive resistance to a more militant response, he spearheaded the difficult decision to take up arms, and was able to persuade his organization to support the new line of action. But when, thirty years on, he deemed that the time had come to move beyond warring polarities toward the negotiation table, again he found the means to stand upon his moral status, push through that decision, and take his organization with him. Repeatedly, he created a role for himself within the ANC's structure and ideological landscape, and then exceeded it. Never doubting he had right on his side, he retained faith in his vision of a nondiscriminatory South Africa through twenty-seven years of incarceration. Eventually he staked a place in his nation's future, as a figure embodying not only justice, but, above all, hope.

## Nelson Mandela: The Story

This book is about the different, interconnected stories, histories, symbols, and values that are referred to using the "famous" name *Nelson Mandela*. Across his life Mandela has filled a rich range of roles: diligent student, city slicker, dashing guerrilla, the world's longest-suffering political prisoner, the millennial savior figure, and so on. He has proved to be a versatile, even postmodern, shape-shifter who at each stage of his career, or his shape-shifting, succeeded in projecting an omnibus appeal. A variety of different constituencies—black nationalists and white communists, rugby players and novelists, world leaders and township dwellers—feeling themselves addressed by him, claimed his emblem for themselves. *Mandela* the tale represents individual journeying and overcoming, but it also *at the same time* tells the collective, many-voiced story of a nation's coming into being.

One of the prominent stories associated with the name Nelson Mandela is inevitably a nationalist story, a *nation's story*. From at least as far back as the midpoint of his presidency, around 1997, Mandela's life narrative was officially elevated as South Africa's main governing tale, its modern myth, as reflected in government school readers and children's cartoon-book histories. His autobiography *Long Walk to Freedom* (1994) itself is not surprisingly styled as a parable in democracy-building. In his biographies, the character and thought of the historical figure are everywhere overlaid with faithful accounts of the political-historical processes in which he was involved. At a more general level, as if to reinforce these representations of the national savior, condensed histories of the twentieth century enshrine the Mandela story as one of the few ethically affirming national tales to emerge from its decades of devastating conflict, often between rival nations.

A short introduction to the career of a figure bulging with this kind of national meaning—not to say heroic symbolization—presents obvious pitfalls, not least the temptation to reproduce the dominant accounts of the secular saint and architect of democracy, where surprisingly few other interpretations exist. The more scholarly biographical studies of Mandela (by Benson, Meer, Sampson, Meredith, Lodge, among others) tend to approach him by his own lights, as, for example, the determined leader of the more militant tendency in the ANC, or the disciplined pilot of his country's destiny. Writing at different historical moments, the biographers differ in their interpretations of his political role, yet do not take issue with his national symbolic significance. For each and every one, Mandela embodies a post-apartheid South Africa. For some, additionally, he is a model, a history with a nationalist moral attached, a pedagogic tale bearing political truth.

For Benson in 1986, writing at the quarter-century point of his incarceration, Mandela is all liberal democrat and responsible party man, a reassuring figure for skeptical Western audiences (and noticeably less radical than in a 1965 collection of articles edited by communist colleague Ruth First). For Meer in 1988, prior to the uncertain hour of his release, he is the consummate patrician, translating familial and ethnic loyalties into a strong network of nationalist affiliation. For Sampson, author of still the most authoritative biography to date, Mandela is in 1999, at the end of his presidency, a shining example of unifying leadership, at once Western and African, "the people's president." For the political historian Lodge, in a cooler though still admiring portrait, Mandela accommodates his charismatic authority to protect South Africa's fragile structures of democratic politics.

As is clear, despite these varying assessments of his politics, each biographer takes the decision to cooperate with a dominant strain in Mandela's own makeup: his emphasis on how a leader's work for the nation molds his own future, and vice versa. This emphasis is reflected, too, in the numerous African leaders' autobiographies published since 1950—by Nkrumah, Azikiwe, Kaunda, among others—to mark the moment of their country's independence, to which group Mandela's obviously belongs. Typically, in most of these narratives, the upward trajectory of the life is amplified by way of a process of metaphorical extension, whereby the story is projected through the exemplary patterns of pilgrimage and metamorphosis. The biographical subject's long period of removal from the world, in jail or in exile, for example, is often followed in the biography by miraculous change or transformation, intended as edifying for readers.

Overdetermined though he may be as the symbol of democratic South Africa, this book cannot sidestep telling the iconic national story figured by the name Nelson Mandela. His achievement is in fact probably incomprehensible outside the historical context of South Africa's freedom struggle, which he did choreograph in several ways. "Mandela's story is central to an understanding of the outcome of the liberation struggle," cultural historian Annie Coombs writes. In other words, this study approaches the national Mandela story conventionally, which is to say chronologically, across two chapters of scene-setting, from a narrative viewpoint which almost inevitably assumes the metaphorical substructure of the long walk and the slow, upward climb. Though the study retraces certain familiar pathways, reinforced by a supporting time line of important dates and events, it attempts to refrain from enshrining Mandela as exemplary. Cross-sectional digressions and sideways pointers to other possible readings will fret the smooth progression of the biographical narrative, anticipating the five topic-based chapters that follow.

Bearing in mind how Mandela has worked throughout as the astute author of his own image, or how he scripted life's text, these later chapters set out to offer a *readerly*, interpretative account of the defining episodes of his biography and key aspects of his approach and achievement. Though frequently sidelined in the biographical studies, these aspects are arguably as important as his national vision in bulwarking his moral and international stature. The alternative windows on Mandela focus, *inter alia*, on his cosmopolitan receptivity to transnational political influences; his protean skills as an urban performer yet projection of an uncompromising masculinity; his "dialogic" prison garden projects; and his international repute as the humanist "icon who outgrew his country" (journalist Shaun Johnson's phrase). In this way the study will in its latter half offer a more interiorized, speculative analysis of Mandela than biographies centered on the towering public figure as a rule provide.

The book's approach via a range of themed (though still chronologically based) readings is informed by anthropologist James Clifford's fruitful idea that an individual life constitutes "a narrative of trans-individual occasions," a crossing point between different inspirations, motivations, traditions, relationships, and roles. The accent will be on how individual histories are formed in relation to one another, in connection with struggles and counter-struggles in other places. True, the crosshatched, sideways, or synchronic perspective may initially seem counterintuitive, given the apparent coherence of the messianic Mandela figure in media and government representations. On reflection, however, it is evident not only that Mandela's life has always been remarkably networked, a busy meeting place of different ideologies and influences (at a time before the 24/7 media access that today's politicians take for granted). It is also true that, as a consummate performer, he has often chosen to operate in several different registers, deploying various personae, either simultaneously or sequentially.

Although Mandela till 1990 led a relatively nation-bound, or indeed island-bound, existence, from the time of his arrival in Johannesburg as a young man in the 1940s, his political project and resistance theory were consistently formed in discussion with colleagues and rivals. Not by nature a contemplative figure, it was these networks that made of him, first, an influential political activist, and later, with the long incarceration, a thoughtful negotiator. Moreover, to the same degree as his life was not confined to a single, nationalist track, so too did his career not fall into discrete phases. There were preoccupations, interests, and responses that either ran across the life or looped back, connecting with earlier phases. The Sophiatown sophisticate of the 1950s returned in the 1990s figure of the debonair statesman. The mission-school student found a new incarnation in the self-disciplined Robben Island letter writer. Far from being limited to a one-directional pathway to freedom, the story of his life crystallizes into clusters of encounters, practices, possibilities, and agendas.

In short, rather than admiring Mandela as such, this book considers the *processes of meaning-making* (including his own) which have caused his achievement to be admired. As a function of its different readings, the discussion will acknowledge that Mandela is in some ways an unlikely figure to have received the kind of adulation that has been showered upon him. It is difficult to think of a more outstanding international figure who was so long out of the public eye, and whose major speeches were so often formulaic and rhetorically cautious.

## Reading Madiba

In order to calibrate his unidirectional national story against his diverse other preoccupations, it is important to pose at this point the specific question of which readings of Mandela present themselves as alternatives to the national myth. What are the other interpretative approaches that cast light on the governing preoccupations of his life? How might we encapsulate the "takes" on the first democratic South African president that draw out his different domains of involvement and appeal?

To begin, alongside the straightforward Mandela-as-new-South-Africa reading, in which he is the chief protagonist within a national drama, there is a *global story* featuring Mandela. Beginning in the 1960s, when his court addresses first drew the world's attention, and resuming in 1988 with his televised seventieth "birthday party" at Wembley, he became in the eyes of others the definition of a world icon. In the media he was constructed, even produced, as a preeminent symbol within an ongoing struggle against exploitation not confined to South Africa. It has been claimed that Mandela is second only to Coca-Cola as the world's most recognizable name. Even if this is only in part true, it certainly is the case that his image appears to resonate with values important to a global community once interconnected by its opposition to apartheid—values including courage, perseverance, justice. In a world where Cold War certainties have collapsed, and the causes that defined the pre-1989 period—communism, anticommunism—have been called into question, Mandela stands for many as a beacon of constancy, vision, new humanism, and hope for change. In this capacity, says Gordimer, he "belongs to the world." Several chapters will touch on the global dimensions of Mandela's ethical-political legacy.

· · · · ·

"Nelson Mandela is *the* famous man, today. One of the few who, in contrast with those who have made our twentieth century infamous of fascism, racism, and war, will mark it as an era that achieved advancement for humanity. So will his name live in history, the context in which he belongs to the world."

*Nadine Gordimer, from* Living in Hope and History *(1990)*

· · · · ·

Mandela's story is also crucially, even quintessentially, the story of an African *quest for modernity*. Here modernity should not be understood as equivalent to colonialism, but as involving a claim to selfhood, to being a subject of history, that is expressed through a process of transposing the vocabularies of modern identity into Africa. Where colonialism impacts on this story is in so far as African subjectivity was routinely excluded from official accounts of European historical progress: in colonial discourse Africa tended to signify either emptiness, a heart of darkness, or mere brute matter, chattel, slaves.

By contrast, any study of Mandela charts a decades-long narrative of black South African political leadership-in-the-making; of how, in a situation of extreme racial discrimination, African individuals and communities set about claiming self-determination, citizenship, and democratic rights. From the time that Mandela the country youth arrived in the city of Johannesburg to find work, he formed a central part of an educated elite that insisted on the right to belong there (as against being confined to the rural hinterland), and to accommodate itself within its public spaces. As Chapters 5 and 6 on Mandela as urban dweller and performer suggest, he boldly created a malleable modern identity by adopting and adapting the city's heterogeneous cultural and political resources. As for his literary counterparts, the writers and journalists of Sophiatown, his legal work, newspaper articles, and speeches took as their task the translation of modernity into local terms, to forge the conditions for the emergence of a black South African citizenry.

In effect, Mandela's story tracks the complicated, inventive ways in which modern life was molded in decolonizing Africa. The uneven introduction of European modernity, whether to rural communities or the Johannesburg townships, encouraged the black elite creatively to deploy different social roles and languages in order at once to question colonial stereotypes *and* assert themselves as agents within their communities. As will become clear, in South Africa as in other once-colonized places, projecting oneself as a modern individual involved a continual shuttling between different frames of cultural reference, a running together of discrepant though temporally coincident interpretations of one's place in history, as Dipesh Chakrabarty describes.

The narrative of Mandela's quest for modernity represents a powerful way of accounting for the layeredness of his life story, for how he managed to assume different, seemingly contradictory positions. At times he crossed a reconstituted concept of Thembu political tradition with the conventions of modern Western democracy; at others he pitted the aggressive, go-getting energies of urban modernity against the primitivist stereotypes that were favored under apartheid. Indeed, Mandela's quest-story carries a particular modern irony. In his case, far from the African being a belated addition to the history of the making of the modern self, he is now regarded by many, even if in an overcompensatory way, as occupying the highpoint of a global, intrinsically modern struggle for self-determination and human rights.

• • • • •

"His release from prison projected an unchallenged, patriarchal voice, a voice rooted in the most intense physical conflict between blacks and whites on this planet, the final frontier of white supremacy on the African continent, out across the relay systems of the black Atlantic."

*Paul Gilroy, from* The Black Atlantic *(1993)*

• • • • •

Seeing Mandela as the choreographer of an adaptive, capacious African modernity correlates with a related reading: one that views many aspects of his political achievement first as a militant and then as a negotiator as definitively *postcolonial*. Mandela's energies have always been devoted to restoring black South Africans to their buried histories of resistance, to overcoming colonial legacies of power by taking over the languages and the laws of that power in order to effect that overcoming: both are essentially postcolonial undertakings. Though he is a politician first and foremost, not an intellectual, his work (the political activism, critical writings, and speeches taken together) presents us with an intensely *practical* discourse of anticolonial resistance: that is to say, with an anti- or postcolonial *theory-in-practice*. His achievement has been to demonstrate how an oppressive situation can be withstood through a process of strategically repeating and exceeding the oppressor's self-justifying discourses of rationality or belonging, as the case may be. As Chapters 7 and 8 explore, Mandela generated late humanist concepts of resistance and reconciliation through his lifelong, always intensely dialogic, political dealings. His work against apartheid represented a continuously evolving anticolonialism.

In recent years, postcolonial criticism has begun to acknowledge the ways in which postcolonial thought has its stimulus and structure in anticolonial practice. Critics like Benita Parry and Robert Young have pointed out that leading postcolonial ideas are generated from the thick of political struggle. This book extends the territory of this criticism by making the case that Mandela adopted and reanimated ideas we can see as being both anti- and postcolonial. By helping to bring into being the new democratic South Africa, he effectively became a theorist-of-a-kind.

True, like Gandhi till quite recently, Mandela's political and ethical achievements are not widely recognized as theoretically significant, for at least two reasons other than his relative contemporaneity. First, in so far as he was, controversially, an advocate of militant resistance for some part of his career, he was preceded in his arguments for armed struggle both by his Communist Party comrades and by the prominent theorist Frantz Fanon. As Chapter 4 on Mandela's influences suggests, Fanon's powerful justification of anticolonial violence is likely to have had a shaping effect on the ANC's shift to armed resistance in 1961. Mandela was no flag-bearer in this respect. Secondly, the relative theoretical invisibility of Mandela is in part also because, unlike Gandhi, he was never as resistant as was the Indian leader to articulating his opposition to the repressive state in the selfsame cultural terms as deployed by that state. He invoked the priority of Europe (if selectively), including its notions of modern progress and "civilized" values, in order to frame his critique of apartheid.

Against his apparent theoretical neglect, this book's postcolonial reading of Mandela, which runs across its second half, will allow us to gain critical purchase precisely on contradictory articulations such as these. If postcolonialism is defined as the attempt by the world's marginalized to lay claim to its centers of meaning, then Mandela's efforts to promote African cultural values and indigenous histories of freedom struggle are unequivocally postcolonial. Yet so, too, was his pragmatic empathy for the rival nationalist position of South Africa's Afrikaner minority in the 1980s—an identification that pushed him toward the risky bid for cross-racial conciliation. For him, intrinsically African qualities of reciprocal brotherhood and consensualism are, at the same time, intensely human qualities: *Africanness* and *humanness* are coextensive, not oppositional. This redemptive inclusiveness represents a definitively postcolonial vision.

The long road to freedom is a never-ending road: with this often-repeated suggestion Mandela ends his autobiography. His life, unfolding in proximity to a lively black literary culture, has spawned many enduring metaphors. Regent's ward, Black Pimpernel, prison cell scholar, master of fate, lifelong pilgrim toward democracy: throughout Mandela has been perceived, and perceived himself, in strongly symbolic and mythic terms, to an extent that justifies, finally, a *literary reading* of his achievement. Indeed, it is safe to say that Mandela has so consistently lived in ways governed by *form-giving images* and overarching *generic patterns* that his life has been itself built into metaphor, as several poems and novels record. If across the 1970s and 1980s apartheid was internationally seen as a timeless referent of iniquity, then the figure who led the struggle against that iniquity has absorbed something of that iconic timelessness.

Sections of the themed chapters that follow, especially Chapters 6 and 7, consider the many figurative aspects of *Mandela*, the story and the icon, and offer speculations on the powerful tendency toward self-symbolization and postmodern performance that marked his adult experience. From the time he became a successful lawyer, then a charismatic nationalist, Mandela set himself up as the realization of his people's expectations. Throughout, he remained acutely aware that power requires symbolism and myth for its elevation, to the extent that he became himself a totem of the totemic values of our age—toleration and liberal democracy.

# TWO

## Scripting a Life: The Early Years

●

ANY ATTEMPT TO NARRATE THE LIFE of Nelson Mandela confronts
the difficulty that to do so is to tell a double-framed story—of South
Africa, and of Mandela in South Africa, in the second half of the twentieth century. As the title of his 1978 collection of speeches *The Struggle
Is My Life* announces, from the time of the 1952 Defiance Campaign,
Mandela's actions were intensively informed by—interactive with and
against—the operations of the South African state. This was publicly
so until 1964; then again, decisively, from 1990; and clandestinely and
covertly in the intervening years.

Indeed, as is often the case in nations reconstituting themselves after
periods of tribulation, the biography of Mandela the First President (or
Praise-dent, as one journalist writes) is now officially held up as the *definitive*

**The Transkei region** of South Africa, where Mandela was born, is bordered on the north by the
province of Natal (now called KwaZulu-Natal), on the east by the Indian Ocean, and on the south
by the Great Kei River.

*history* of the *new South Africa's coming into being.* For modern nationalism it is generally true to say that a nation's integrity is recognized both by its citizens and the wider community of nations through the medium of a rallying tale recounting how it was constituted. In South Africa that preeminent story is Nelson's story. As for other national heroes—Thomas Jefferson, Napoleon, Jawaharlal Nehru—Mandela's life story and character have been built up as icons of national progress and virtue.

Worshipful nationalist biography or hagiography is perhaps especially acute when the nation, as in the case of South Africa, has been born, or in fact twice-born, out of racial conflict and repression. The 1910 Union of South Africa was forged on the basis of a fragile unity of Afrikaners and English-speaking whites after the Anglo-Boer War (1899–1902)—the culmination of a series of wars over land and resources fought between British and Dutch settlers and indigenous black populations across the nineteenth century. The unified settler colony's underlying geography and overarching state structures were from the start strongly racialized, and in subsequent decades the Afrikaner's sense of marginalization by the British-descended settlers only fueled their already defensive nationalism. In 1948 the reformed Afrikaner Nationalist Party won victory on the ticket of founding a white-dominated state. As Mandela himself was to recognize, the history of twentieth-century South Africa was profoundly shaped by the fierce contest between two nationalisms, Afrikaner and African, for the "same piece of earth."

A second, related yet separate, difficulty with recounting Mandela's life concerns the generic, especially allegorical, patterns through which his story tends to be narrated. In all of the biographies bar none, the authors of Mandela the Life assume a more or less onward-and-upward trajectory, fitting the overarching motif of a journey or pilgrimage signaled in his autobiography's title. This suggests that the "long walk to freedom" may be tough and uphill but it begins with a rural idyll, proceeds through setbacks and difficulties, and ends, as does that of Christian in Bunyan's *The Pilgrim's Progress* (1678), with the achievement of the Celestial City, the free, democratic nation. The steady-climb metaphor subtends the number of beginner's guides widely available in South Africa and beyond, including the soft-focus *Madiba* by Lionel Maxim, the "They Fought for Freedom" and "Famous Lives" series contributions, and the Nelson Mandela Foundation's own "Madiba Legacy" comic-book series. But the standard biographies, too—Meer's, Sampson's, Meredith's—at times intermittently, yet also unmistakably, adopt the ready-made journey motif.

The ubiquity of the life-journey trope in Nelson's story pertains not only to the aura that accrued over the prison years to *No Easy Walk to Freedom*: the Nehru-inspired title of his 1965 collection of speeches which was confirmed in the title of his later autobiography. It also attaches closely to the prevalence of ideas of redemptive onward journeying in African writing generally, which links with the influential role played by Bunyan's *The Pilgrim's Progress* in the mission-school education of many African writers, intellectuals, and politicians, as Isabel Hofmeyr's insightful *The Portable Bunyan* explains. Christian's story appealed powerfully to young African readers fortified by the values of community and hard work inculcated through their rural, traditional, often Christianized childhoods, even as they battled to forge self-reliance in a context inimical to black opportunity. The journey framework offered African writers a symbolic space within which to plot patterns of incremental self-improvement and progress (whether toward modernity or back to tradition). Any number of autobiographical African *Bildungsroman* appearing from the 1940s onward follow the same trajectory: Camara Laye's *L'enfant noir* (1954), Mphahlele's *Down Second Avenue* (1959), Achebe's *No Longer at Ease* (1960), Ngugi's *Weep Not, Child* (1964).

As this suggests, embedding the influential "long road" motifs, Mandela's story exhibits, too, a recognizable *typicality*, underpinned by a dominant teleology of political growth with liberation as its goal. By recounting a steady progression toward freedom and modernity, despite inevitable setbacks, the life story runs in parallel with the largely masculine, unidirectional narrative of resistance and overcoming as it has been played out in Africa and elsewhere in the once-colonized world. As such, his tale shares common ground with the biographies and memoirs, too, of his colleagues Walter Sisulu, Oliver Tambo, and Albert Luthuli.

Beginning with the ANC's regeneration through the Youth League in the 1940s, the iconic Mandela life story traces a path through the "festive activism" of the 1950s, the 1960s' years of incarceration and exile, the resurgent militancy of the post-1976 period, and the 1990s' slow strategizing and achievement of liberation. The youth raised in a chiefly Thembu household becomes the pioneering black lawyer and political leader who finally emerges, after twenty-seven desert years, as the new South Africa's first democratic president. The enmeshing of the models of upward mobility with motifs of travel and pilgrimage is further emphasized in Mandela's autobiography by the important role played there by transformative journeys. On the first drive to school in Jongintaba's Ford, on the long car ride to Johannesburg, city of electric light, on his 1962 trip around Africa, Nelson the protagonist of the tale repeatedly has his aspirations encouraged and confirmed. The journey conforms to a trope of progress driven, as is Christian of *The Pilgrim's Progress*, by "dedicated and principled effort." Throughout, Mandela's vision of life has been of an uphill path climbed by dint of discipline and hard work.

• • • • •

"With the mutilation and decline of the conquered tribe a new shaman or artist struggles to emerge who finds himself moving along the knife-edge of change. He has been, as it were, cross-fertilized by victor and victim and a powerful need arises to invoke the lost generations, in a new, creative, visionary light. It is a task which is profoundly personal (and archetypal) and, therefore, accompanying an enormous potency for change—for vision into resources—runs the danger of self-enactment or hubris."

*Wilson Harris, from* Explorations *(1981)*

• • • • •

This book's two different approaches, the one founded on the teleological pathway, the other topic-based, focused on the diffuse processes shaping a life, operate in contrastive ways, though always in relation to one another. The cross-section studies in the key phases of his subjectivity—examining his "Gandhian" makeup or cosmopolitan selfhood—can best be appreciated in their complexity when mapped against the spinal life narrative covered in this and the next chapter, with the watershed moment of incarceration serving as the dividing line between them.

## The Young Mandela

Rolihlahla Mandela was born on July 18, 1918, in the hamlet of Mvezo in the Transkei, the eastern region of the present-day Eastern Cape province, a hilly landscape of great loveliness after rain, and of intense poverty. The Transkei, once the terrain of the widely dispersed isiXhosa-speaking peoples, comprising twelve chieftaincies including the Thembu, was at the time a peasant reserve, the largest area in South Africa where, under the 1913 Land Act restrictions, Africans could still collectively own land. Though the Thembu royalty had generally steered clear of involvement in the vicious nineteenth-century Frontier or Xhosa Wars (and had at times sided with the British), Mandela as a youth would have witnessed how the society around him remained scarred by the painful legacy of these conflicts. Sparked by British colonial encroachment, and fought on and around Xhosa lands for over a century from the 1770s, the Frontier Wars had left the people divided and dispossessed, and smarting at their loss of independence. The Xhosa mourned, too, the loss of their live-stock following the mass panic of the 1856–7 Cattle Killings (though the Thembu again were left relatively unscathed). Much later on, between 1976 and 1994, Transkei held the dubious status of being the apartheid state's first notionally independent black homeland under Mandela's rela-tive, Chief Kaiser Matanzima.

Mandela was born into a high-ranking family of the Xhosa-speaking Thembu chieftaincy. This made him keenly aware from childhood of the stain to ancestral honor—yet proud legacy of resistance and self-reliance—that the Frontier conflicts with the British represented, as the preambles to his 1962 and 1964 addresses to the court both emphasize. In his childhood and youth he was at key points reminded of the lost glories of the African past, especially of the Xhosa-speaking nations. He remembered Chief Joyi, a prominent elder, railing against the white man's injustices in his guardian's courtyard. At his circumcision, Chief Meligqili spoke a litany for the dying flower of the Xhosa peoples, "slaves in our own land." And when the Xhosa poet S. E. Krune Mqhayi paid a visit to Mandela's school Healdtown wearing traditional dress, he recited one of his dramatic poems based on *isibongi* (praise-songs) in which he bestirred the students to cast off "foreign notions."

Rolihlahla's mother, Nonqaphi Nosekeni (Fanny after her conversion to Methodism at Qunu), was the third wife of four of Gadla Henry Mpakhanyiswa, the tall, stern headman of the Mvezo area, counselor to Thembuland's paramount chief David Dalindyebo. A descendant of a minor house (Ixhiba) of the royal lineage of the Thembus, within a polygamous system in which birth order translated into status, Gadla Henry was not permitted to hold high office, but none the less was granted privilege by occupying the position of counselor. Mandela, too, though his father's fourth son, seems to have been preferred due to his mother's favored status. His *sense of entitlement* as a royal, though a minor one, and his mother's firstborn (followed by three sisters), early on bequeathed to him the conviction that he, too, was headed for the role of chief's advisor. This profound sense that "roots were . . . destiny" would remain with him for many years before he was able to stand back and view it more critically.

When the young Mandela was around two years old, a local white magistrate charged Gadla Henry with insubordination for having disregarded his orders. Already at this point a white grid of authority tightly enmeshed the indigenous structures of Transkei power. Gadla Henry was dismissed as headman and, losing income as well as status, was forced to move Nosekeni's branch of the family to Qunu village, located on the motorway from Durban to the Cape, where Mandela's retirement house now stands.

At Qunu, the young Mandela was singled out by the influential, Westernized Mbekela brothers as a bright child with good prospects. He was baptized a Methodist and, aged eight, sent to the village school. He attended wearing a cutoff pair of his father's trousers, his first garment of this kind, and experienced all at once the aura that comes with wearing the right costume: "being dressed properly." This was later confirmed in his favorite household task of pressing his guardian's suits. Although at this point he spoke no English, his teacher Miss Mdingane gave him his for-whites-pronounceable "English" name, Nelson—a Christian name being a customary tag for Africans in colonial society, while also of course serving as a marker of their belief. Outside the classroom he enjoyed a carefree pastoral childhood of herding, outdoor games, and fireside tales. In these years he laid down an appreciation of "the veldt, the great open spaces, the simple beauty of nature, and the pure line of the horizon," images that would sustain him in prison. These words, written in a letter to his friend Frieda Matthews, surface in almost the same form in his autobiography.

In 1927 Mandela's father died of a lung disease, probably tuberculosis, having not long before entrusted his promising youngest son to the Thembu regent Jongintaba Dalindyebo's house to be further educated and "prepared for a wide world." Feeling "cut adrift," at once awestruck and bewildered, Mandela carrying a tin trunk accompanied his mother to Mqhekezweni, Jongintaba's impressive "Great Place," a large compound comprising African huts and Western-style houses. Here, without undue fuss, she handed him over to the care of the man who would from then on, for over a decade, act as his guardian and the shaper of his aspirations. Thereafter her son would see her only infrequently, something that Mandela later regretted and mourned.

The boy Nelson quickly developed a close bond with his guardian's extrovert, slightly older son, Justice Bambilanga, and joined with him in his activities—churchgoing, ballroom dancing, and reading the *Chambers English Reader* at school. Yet, despite the stimulation that this "sophisticated," prosperous new homestead with its wooden floorboards and Jongintaba's "majestic" Ford V8 car offered, Nelson would always experience a keen sense of abandonment, often translated when in a group into an air of lofty distance, a shield against expressing grief. He had within only a few weeks lost his two closest family ties, his mother and father, and though he was known during these years as a prankster, some of the teases involved petty theft (corn, pigs, cattle) and bed-hopping forced by bed-wetting, which suggests a certain level of insecurity. He fitted the mold of a late developer—serious, uncertain, mindful to a fault of his mentor's injunctions. Surely yet quite slowly he developed confidence at school.

Among his most formative experiences at the Great Place was the opportunity he had to observe customary *consensual democracy* at work, in the form of Jongintaba's on-the-job chieftaincy. Nelson watched how the all-male, open-air tribal meetings were conducted: the enactment of fellowship through discussion; Jongintaba's attentive listening to the chiefs' cases; his attempts at the end of the meeting to forge unanimity. This spectacle of working toward consensus had, according to *Long Walk to Freedom*, a shaping effect on Mandela's later style of leadership. The claim is plausible to a degree. At this stage, it is important to remember, Mandela had as yet had little or no contact with the world of white authority whereas, by contrast, the manner in which his guardian disposed of his power had till now entirely determined his view of the world.

Any retrospective construction, as in *Long Walk to Freedom* and the biographies based on it, is subject to a certain amount of allegorical inflation, especially at a time, the mid-1990s, when the ideal of African social harmony carried particular symbolic resonance. It is evident that Mandela's respect for liberal or what he calls "ordinary democracy" has at many points in his career been equally as strong as, if not stronger than, his allegiance to consensual decision-making, or susceptibility to the powerful mythic imagery of precolonial village democracy. However, what the autobiographical account does make clear is that the long-winded yet wisely choreographed meetings in the chief's courtyard represented an important lesson for the young Mandela in how agreement between competing views might be achieved: how patrimonial loyalties and clan obligations might be weighed against one another. While in an ordinary democracy the will of the majority was asserted, in this traditional situation all constituencies were heard and the leader paid heed to all. Yet this did not mean that the two different modes could not be made to cooperate. Notwithstanding the absence of women, the tribal meeting represented a relatively pure dramatization, according to Mandela, of the traditional African ideal of *ubuntu*—mutual responsibility and community—at work, to which apartheid's exclusions stood in diametrical opposition.

## Schooling

In early 1934, when Mandela was sixteen, his guardian arranged an initiation school for his son Justice, which included a group of other adolescent boys, among them his ward. Initiation for Xhosa youths at this time meant a retreat into the country with fellow initiates for a three-week period, circumcision, the giving of a new name (for Mandela, Dalibhunga, "the founder of the ruling body"), the burning of old garments, and the wearing of an all-body white-clay mask. Mandela's autobiographical account of this period, which grew in importance to him with time, oscillates between the dreams of a future of wealth and status which the experience triggered, and of a nagging sense of inadequacy, of not yet being "a man" despite being officially nominated as such.

Not long after the initiation, Jongintaba sent Mandela to Clarkebury Boarding Institute, a coeducational Methodist secondary school built on land given to the church by their ancestor King Ngubengcuka some hundred years before. As was the case throughout colonial Africa, mission schools like Clarkebury formed one of the primary agents of colonial expansion, often driven by universalist Christian (sometimes Social Darwinist) ideas concerning the degrees of civilization and possible redemption attainable by different peoples or races. However, there were among them more liberal, independent-minded institutions, including within the Methodist missionary service influential in the Transkei, where emphasis was laid on salvation as contingent upon dedication and hard work.

At Clarkebury, Mandela soon discovered that any claim he might make to special status as a lesser royal would be given short shrift, as many fellow students, equally well connected, regarded him as a country yokel, barely able to walk about in shoes. Presided over by the severe Reverend Cecil Harris, the school's regime was strict, even militaristic, yet generally fair. Mandela was given a single special privilege as the regent's ward: instead of the usual manual outdoor duties expected of students, he was allowed to tend the Harrises' garden. Here, as well as discovering his lifelong love of raising plants, he opened a unique window onto the private life of a white person, and this almost immediately after meeting them: a rare insight for a black South African youth at this time. Relying on his exceptionally retentive memory, Mandela at Clarkebury obtained his "middle school" diploma or Junior Certificate in two rather than the usual three years.

In 1937 Mandela moved on to Healdtown College, a Methodist senior school, where he matriculated. The school was built close to Fort Beaufort, one of the important British outposts in the Xhosa wars. To reach it, traveling by car, train, and on foot, Mandela for the first time crossed the great Kei River, a key frontier in those same wars. The land was laden with reminders, to quote the poet Mqhayi (whom he was soon to meet), of how the "metal wire" of Europe had strangled and overwhelmed the "*assegai*" of African strength and pride.

At Healdtown, Xhosa youths like Mandela, as well as a proportion of students from neighboring communities or tribes, were trained to become "black Englishmen" (his own phrase), once again following an austere Victorian regime that inculcated *self-restraint* and *hard work*. Their first bell was at 6:00 a.m., lights-out at 9:30 p.m.: their diet comprised bread, maize starch, and water. Yet Mandela took relatively easily to this discipline and found that maintaining it helped him imbibe more effectively what he was taught. In later years he would declare himself always still an Anglophile, a lifelong admirer of English political institutions and manners.

He continued as at Clarkebury to enjoy sports of different kinds, excelling in particular at long-distance running, which afforded him, he said, a stimulating "discipline and solitariness," to the extent that he continued this sport into his university years. As will be evident from his story so far, the self-mastery that Mandela had acquired in order to deal with his personal losses was strongly underpinned within the strict institutional contexts of his boarding schools. By the time he was ready to become a political leader, the qualities of self-discipline, perseverance, and dedication had come to seem to him not only second nature, but inalienable attributes for anyone in authority.

Intent on "grooming" Mandela "for success in the world," Jongintaba in 1939 obtained a scholarship from the Transkei authorities for his ward to continue his studies at the University of Fort Hare, at this time the most prestigious tertiary educational institution for black Africans south of the equator. Although his cousin Justice had until now preceded him up the school ladder, Mandela would from here on outstrip him. He arrived at university wearing a wristwatch and a new three-piece suit with wide lapels, bought for him by his guardian. Although a recent interview gives an earlier date for the photograph in which he sports these new clothes, the suit even so represented his simultaneous introduction to the seductions of Western dress—presenting himself as a "black Englishman"—*and* to the most stimulating intellectual environment he had yet encountered.

Fort Hare had opened in 1916 as Native Central College, built on land donated by the Methodist mission of Lovedale. Only two decades on, it had, under the disciplinarian directorship of Dr. Alexander Kerr, become a premier training ground for the tiny black South African middle class. Still a Xhosa at heart, Mandela was now thrust into a vibrant intercultural social network, comprising the representatives of southern Africa's leading black families (the Jabavus and Bokwes), and the gifted sons of poorer, less fortunate communities, like Oliver Tambo. Together, they prefigured the diverse black South African nation of the future.

Mandela set out to study toward a combined BA degree in his now-chosen career of native administration, taking such subjects as history, anthropology, and law from some of the leading African scholars of the day, including Professors Z. K. Matthews and D. D. T. Jabavu. He and his cohort were strongly motivated by their sense of their special status as an elite who, in the words of "Z. K.," would achieve success "through hard work and moderation," as the African-American Booker T. Washington had advised. By and large, however, their pride in themselves was not expressed politically. Indeed, their position in many ways depended on their still-uncritical support for the status quo. With the beginning of the Second World War, the students declared themselves "ardent" Allied supporters, applauding the one-time Boer general Jan Smuts, the guest speaker at the University's 1940 graduation ceremony, for his efforts in taking South Africa into the war. By contrast, the ANC was an organization "vaguely heard of," seemingly lost in the past, though Z. K., an ANC activist, had protested against the Cape Province's abrogation of the black vote. Despite the fact that Mandela in these years experienced his first openly racial incidents, and befriended people from various different backgrounds, nationalist and moderate, at this point strongly expressed political associations made him feel profoundly confused.

Toward the end of his second year at Fort Hare, a conflict broke out between students and staff on the grounds of the ill treatment of a canteen worker, exacerbated by an earlier protest over food. This development, which abruptly ended the first phase of Mandela's university career, eventually proved a milestone on the road toward his politicization. The sequence of what actually transpired differs between the various biographical accounts. Despite the claims to the contrary in his autobiography, on balance it seems the case that Mandela was *not* part of the student council that called for an SRC election boycott in response to the canteen incident. Instead, already elected to the council by a small minority, he followed a more lonely road of protest by refusing to take up his position, which prompted Kerr to suspend him. With this setback if anything steeling his determination, he returned home to face a furious Jongintaba, who insisted he go back to complete his degree.

A prolonged standoff between regent and ward was avoided by a second hammer-blow decision that may or may not have been sparked by the first. Jongintaba, a traditional patriarch at heart, that summer arranged marriages for both Justice and his ward, going so far as to pay *lobola* (bride price) for the two women concerned. In spite of all he knew he owed his guardian, Mandela, together with his cousin, decided that he could not comply with a tradition imposed without consultation. Within only a few days the two young men took steps to escape to the space of black opportunity that was Johannesburg, the burgeoning former mining town, so embarking on the big-city pilgrimage already traced by many of their compatriots, black and white. In the period 1936–46, when the two made their journey, Johannesburg's black population, encouraged by the relaxed influx controls of the war period, increased by tens of thousands.

Under Jongintaba's suspicious eye, the two young men organized their escape in secret, forced to sell his oxen to raise money for their rail fare, and to bluster their way through pass controls. (Passes were ID-type documents regulating black movement around the country: at this point black men alone were required to carry them.) On the final leg of their trip, they were driven in the car of a white contact and, that night, confronted the revelation of massed electric light that was Johannesburg. Although this seemed like the fulfillment of a long journey, in reality, Mandela wrote, it was "the very beginning of a much longer and more trying one." Yet, aside from his sense of indebtedness to his guardian, this step into a new future was one that he felt more than ready to take. No doubt acting from the feeling of detachment from established loyalties that the early disintegration of his family home had bequeathed, and from his belief in his own capacity to master self and destiny, Mandela appears to have been prepared to sever his lineage obligations virtually overnight. He was keen boldly to step forward as a modern subject, open to the independent new ways of fashioning an identity that the city offered.

The woman who gave the two young men the paid-for lift from Queenstown to Johannesburg that would change their lives was one of the first white people, other than teachers and their wives, to whom Mandela had ever talked at any length. In closing this section tracking his transition into young adulthood, it is worth asking how it was that someone like him, growing up in a land striated with signs of white colonization and African destitution, had up till now avoided feelings of racial inferiority and resentment as a black person. After all, both the elegiac voices of leading community elders, and the generalized nationalist histories of his BA studies, had poignantly reminded him of his people's losses, of the pitched "wars fought . . . in defense of the fatherland," as he said in his 1964 Rivonia speech.

A colonial context based on racial oppression generates pathologies in both the black consciousness and the white, as postcolonial theory describes. This was perhaps nowhere more evident than in South Africa, where a dominant ideology of white supremacy informed all state

**Mandela's move to** Johannesburg in 1941 was the first step in his long journey from the confines of tribal tradition to the wider opportunities of the world at large. This photograph of Rissik Street in downtown Johannesburg was taken in 1940.

policy. As W. E. B. DuBois said of African America in 1903, within a colonial system black people "always [look] at [themselves] through the eyes of others . . . measuring [their] soul by the tape of a world that looks on in amused contempt and pity." For 1950s South African writer Can Themba, also Fort Hare-educated, "the burden of the white man's crime against my personality . . . negatives all the brilliance of intellect. . . . The whole bloody ethos still asphyxiates me." Did Mandela not share such feelings of lack, of falling short when measured by the standards of the white world? How did he avoid the asphyxiating burden of *black negation*, that "intense intrapsychic pain" produced when the oppressed internalize the oppressor's perceptions, in the influential formulation of anticolonial analyst Frantz Fanon?

The answer to these questions is complicated, but is probably contained in the fact of Mandela's privileged upbringing in a relatively sheltered rural environment of well-off peasant farmers. His guardian's status more than compensated for his father's loss of prestige, and he grew up expecting to partake in the environment of entitlement and self-possession that surrounded the Thembu aristocracy. In Jongintaba's courtyard, black institutions of authority operated with success despite colonialism, and white institutions existed at a distance for much of the time. As Mandela writes, the regent treated any white traders and government officials who visited "on equal terms as they did him."

Until he arrived in Johannesburg, therefore, Mandela, effectively a member of two overlapping elites, Thembu and mission school, would only rarely have been the object of derogatory white eyes. Even then, at both school and university, his self-perception was buttressed by his membership of different communities of independent black minds. Throughout, within the liberal if hierarchical environments of his

Methodist colleges and then of Fort Hare, the students' sense of election was in the main encouraged. In this emerging public sphere, as one commentator describes, they were free to try out a range of different vocabularies of modern progress through which to define themselves, regardless of the color of their skin. Here, as long as an individual was prepared to work hard, rewards, whether worldly or spiritual, would be theirs. Hence Mandela's often relentless exhortation of his own children to show drive and ambition, and make something of their lives.

Mandela's self-possession as a modern subject was to be tested in the new urban environment of Johannesburg, as when he encountered the segregated tea-tray arrangements at his first law office workplace. His self-confidence was sufficiently embedded, however, not to be seriously threatened. As Gordimer, among others, observes, this secure sense of self in all likelihood also explains how it is that he emerged from his years of incarceration without acrimony. This, and the support he enjoyed throughout from a strong network of friends and contacts. Moreover, in Johannesburg, because of the war situation, longer vistas of opportunity were presented to black men than had been the case hitherto.

## Big-City Life

Mandela's first city job was as a mine compound policeman, Justice's as a clerk, which positions they secured using their Thembu contacts. The same network entrapped them, however, when an infuriated Jongintaba wrote to have them fired. Through a relative with whom he lived for a while, Mandela then obtained an introduction to Xhosa "home boy" Walter Sisulu (1912–2003), a well-connected real estate agent working off Commissioner Street in central Johannesburg and already a socialist-leaning ANC member. The meeting with this remarkable man—always confident and capable despite lacking Mandela's social status, proudly African regardless of his mixed-race parentage—fundamentally changed the younger man's life.

Sisulu, for his part, appears to have been struck by something at once reassuring and impressive in Mandela's presence. On the strength of their very brief acquaintance, he set his new friend up as an office worker and prospective articled clerk in the white Jewish legal firm of Witkin, Sidelsky and Eidelman, with Lazar Sidelsky as his "courtly" mentor. This work, it was hoped, would become Mandela's springboard to returning to university for further legal studies. His education to date, he now felt, was "hardly . . . relevant" in a context where his new cohorts, lacking degrees, spoke better English and were more city-wise.

His autobiography does not explicitly address why he decided on the law, apart from the contingencies of meeting Sisulu. However, the connection between the roles of native administrator, conventionally a rural posting, and of lawyer, the equivalent city profession, is self-evident. Notwithstanding the law's limited role in guarding civil liberties in South Africa, the courts presented Mandela with a space where, as in Jongintaba's courtyard, people's conflicting interests, exacerbated by their segregated environment, might be deliberated, if not resolved. Like his Indian counterpart Gandhi, Mandela had already at this early stage developed a marked respect for the ideals of *justice* and *arbitration*.

Living first in the unlit or "Dark City" of Alexandra, later in the expanding, redbrick township of Orlando, Mandela was thrown into the thick of the black struggle for urban survival and political self-reliance. (The charged atmosphere of these formative city years is detailed in Chapter 5.) With Jongintaba's death, his allowance ceased (it had been restored following a reconciliation), and this cast the former ward upon the generosity of acquaintances and loans from charitable groups. He walked to save bus-fare money and wore the same suit every day, yet managed to impress his legal firm with his disciplined commitment to his work.

In 1943, the same year that he began regularly to attend ANC meetings along with radical fellow clerk Gaur Radebe, he enrolled for a part-time LL.B. degree at the largely white University of the Witwatersrand. He persisted with these studies alongside his clerkship and political work, often under difficult conditions. Fellow students like Ruth First remembered him during this period as reserved, immaculately dressed, and "very conscious of his blackness" (acutely perhaps for the first time). In 1944 he married the nurse Evelyn Mase, a devout, apolitical woman, mother to four of his children, who for fourteen years provided him with the secure family base from which to organize himself as a radical nationalist. His many rival commitments were, however, inimical to concentrated study. In 1949 he failed his final law examination and was forced to complete his legal training through on-the-job professional practice.

**In December of 1951,** Mandela attended an African National Congress conference in Bloemfontein, South Africa, with, among others, fellow activist Ruth First (1925–82), seen at right in this photograph.

Mandela's growth into political awareness was occasioned, he later recognized, not by an "epiphany" racial incident but rather by the "thousand indignities" he witnessed every day on Johannesburg's streets. Following the success of the Radebe-led 1943 bus boycott, which demonstrated the power of mass action, he discovered himself to be "devoted" to the liberation of his people. Via contacts at work, he met South African Communist Party (SACP) members like Michael Harmel, J. B. Marks, and Moses Kotane, and was introduced to "illuminating" new modes of social analysis, most particularly, he remembered, dialectical materialist theories of revolutionary change. Harmel is likely to have talked him through the emerging Marxist thesis of internal colonialism, as it was on the basis of communist hospitality to national liberation movements that Mandela later accepted SACP-ANC collaboration. (In brief, the thesis held that the class system in a colonized context like South Africa was underdeveloped, with oppression being at once race- and class-based, which meant that socialists should forge alliances with African nationalists.)

Though a heckler at Communist meetings in the 1940s, Mandela at times attended the Communist Party night school in Fox Street and, some years later, in 1950, put himself through a reading program in the Marxist canon, encouraged by Harmel. Comparatively speaking, however, Sisulu pursued a consistently more radical edge in his thinking, formally joining the reconstituted underground Communist Party in 1953, which Mandela never did. From the latter's viewpoint, as a nationalist suspicious of the "foreignness" to Africa of communism, a place was always to be reserved at the liberation table for the black bourgeoisie. (This was reflected in his political writing, though the paragraphs in question were edited from the 1965 edition of his articles.)

As things turned out, Mandela joined the ANC at a time of rein-vigorated ferment in the organization, stirred up to a considerable extent by his new companions Sisulu and Radebe, as well as the brilliant, pas-sionately nationalist Anton Lembede. Founded in 1912 by Pixley ka Seme, Sol Plaatje, and John Dube as a political organization to campaign for native land rights, the ANC had by the late 1930s become a nonconfronta-tional, if not almost dormant, political organization, whose activities, such as they were, focused mainly on petitioning. A new period in its fortunes was inaugurated with the election in 1940 of the energetic Alfred Xuma. He presided over the younger members' successful call at the 1943 annual conference for the formation of a Youth League based on Africanist ideas and nonhierarchical grassroots structures, as well as for a change to the constitution to accord full equality to women members.

The ANC Youth League (ANCYL), one of the most important forces to shape South African politics in the second half of the twentieth century, was formally launched at the Bantu Men's Social Center in Eloff Street in early 1944. Tapping the new spirit of nationalism emerging among the African masses during the war period, the ANCYL manifesto called for the African to "determine his future by his own efforts." On the back of Mandela's concentrated work in helping to set up the League, he was in 1947 elected to the Transvaal provincial ANC executive, and in 1948 became ANCYL Secretary with the responsibility of organizing new branches and galvanizing recruitment.

The ANCYL's response to the 1948 victory of the Afrikaner National Party on an apartheid ticket (to bring racial segregation into law) was to launch in 1949 a "Program of Action," aiming to push for mass protests on Gandhian lines, as Mandela explained in the *African Lodestar* magazine. Confronted with the government's repressive new legislation, he was, like his colleagues A. P. Mda, Tambo, and Sisulu, concerned to put the "machinery" of African liberation in order (the term was Sisulu's). In late 1949, the League succeeded in its plan of gaining control of the ANC executive by ousting the by-now-too-cautious Xuma in favor of the seemingly more malleable Dr. James Moroka, and soon thereafter Mandela was co-opted onto the national executive in Xuma's place. In 1950, he was elected ANCYL President to replace Mda, who had been forced to resign due to illness.

Although Mandela continued to disagree with Sisulu as late as 1950 over his support for communists and Indians, between the May Day protests that year, disrupted by police, and the subsequent June 26 Day of Mourning, organized by a joint nationalist-communist, Indian-African committee, he underwent an important change of heart. His respect for the high level of organization that distinguished these other groups appears to have translated into a more pragmatic approach to forging alliances with them. This was vividly exemplified in the 1952 Defiance Campaign, launched to turn "non-European unity" into a living force against "fascism," in Mandela's words. The development, for which he acted as volunteer-in-chief, is fully sketched in Chapter 4 on his political and intellectual influences.

1952 represented a key year in Mandela's career. Even though many local ANC branches were noticeably self-motivated in their participation in Defiance, the success of the mass campaign, and the fact that crowds *across* the country marched *nonviolently* against apartheid legislation, gave him a prominent public profile, unmatched by others of his generation. The Defiance Campaign proved decisive, too, in shaping the ANC's broad-church politics for the rest of the decade. In his efforts to recruit support, Mandela personally felt he had developed a new confidence as a "freedom fighter": "the white man had felt the power of my punches and I could walk upright like a man."

## The Ongoing Impact of Defiance

From the early 1950s onward, Mandela's leadership skills, complemented by his formal legal training and gift for forging friendships across various color bars, were in constant demand. His comrades were aware that Congress needed a rallying leader-figure at its head and appear to have collaborated even in these Defiance years in burnishing his charismatic image. He qualified as an attorney in the same year that he became a public political presence, and joined with Fort Hare fellow graduate Oliver Tambo in August 1952 in establishing South Africa's first black-owned law office, located on Fox Street in downtown Johannesburg. He came to be well known for his assertive, theatrical performances in court, which turned the busy legal practice into a commercial success.

· · · · ·

"You can recognize an authentic inheritor in the one who conserves and reproduces, but also in the one who respects the logic of the legacy enough to turn it upon occasion against those who claim to be its guardians."

*Jacques Derrida, from "The Laws of Reflection:*
*Nelson Mandela, In Admiration" (1987)*

· · · · ·

In any political action, as several contemporaries noted, Mandela always worked to reconcile his tendency to gravitate to an aloof if commanding position with his conviction that a leader should be identified with his people's interests. This duality is epitomized in his 1950s formulation of the so-called M-Plan or Mandela plan—a network structure of tight-knit cells devised for the ANC in the event that the organization was banned. Mandela always claimed credit for inaugurating the plan (and did in fact advocate it widely): this accorded with his concern to be wholeheartedly bound up with his Congress. Yet, as biographer Tom Lodge contends, he appears initially to have acquired the idea from modes of grassroots organization in the Eastern Cape; in other words, through cautious, "regal" observation from the sidelines. His prison years would reinforce his characteristic distanced stance, though it was balanced with a steady endorsement of open, democratic structures of engagement and agreement. Throughout the Johannesburg period and beyond, strong horizontal relations with comrades and colleagues calibrated Mandela's "vertical" patrician obligations.

The government responded to the threat to state security represented by the Defiance Campaign with "drastic" measures: raids, arrests, and penalties against unconstitutional action. In July 1952, Mandela was arrested on a charge of violating the Suppression of Communism Act and, when charged, given a suspended sentence for his role in the campaign. Not long thereafter, coinciding with the election of Christian pacifist Chief Albert Luthuli as ANC president, a banning order confined him to the Johannesburg magisterial district for a six-month period, preventing him from making public speeches and forcing him to give up his important new post of Transvaal ANC president. This represented the beginning of ten years of repeated arrests and bannings, interspersed with short "free" periods dodging the police.

In 1954 Mandela was forced to contest a Transvaal Law Society petition that he be struck from the roll of attorneys on account of his "law-breaking" activities. His efforts in this regard were successful, but from this time onward his respect for the rule of law would be repeatedly tested by the state's concern to treat him as an "unconvicted criminal," to quote from his 1962 trial statement. Despite his banning, he participated in a low-key way in the agitation against the Sophiatown removals, all the while coming to the grim realization that the peaceful protests would, tragically, not succeed in beating the government; neither now, nor on any future occasion. Not long after his first banning order expired his frustration erupted in an unusually militant speech given in Sophiatown's Freedom Square, in which he conceded, to the crowd's delight, that nonviolence could not overturn "a white minority regime bent on retaining power at any cost."

In the polarized context of the deepening Cold War, with the government defining all opposition as "statutory communism" and cementing its policy of full geographic apartheid, the ANC's countervailing response was steadily to widen the basis of the struggle by consolidating the multiracial, intercultural coalition it could potentially represent. In 1955 this widening took the form of a National Convention entrusted with the task of drafting a Freedom Charter, a liberal-humanist *and* socialist constitution that would sketch the shape of a future South Africa and, it was hoped, ditch racialized politics for good. Deploying the same networks and outreach initiatives as had the Defiance Campaign, drafts of the Charter were discussed in ANC, Indian National Congress, and (white) Congress of Democrats meetings around the country and approved at a vast Congress of the People meeting at Kliptown near Johannesburg on June 26–27, 1955. Mandela, under his second banning order, watched from a distance. He was by now making extensive use of journalism to participate in the public debate about the Charter and in a June 1956 *Liberation* article endorsed its keynotes: the *full transfer of power* to "the people" and *state nationalization*.

In December 1956, the government responded in its most heavy-handed way yet to the resistance movement building in the country, by arresting key participants in the Defiance Campaign and Congress of the People, 156 in total, including Mandela and representing all races, and then charging them with high treason. The protracted Treason Trial that followed (first in the Johannesburg Drill Hall, then in the Pretoria Old Synagogue) whittled the original number of accused down to thirty, and crippled Mandela and Tambo's law practice, as well as the livelihoods of many other accused. Yet the trial process at first turned out to be interpersonally productive: meetings were facilitated between activists from around the country, and different race groups, usually divided into their separate political organizations, discovered a surprising sense of solidarity-in-resistance.

**This photograph, taken on December 19, 1956,** shows crowds outside Drill Hall in Johannesburg as prisoners were brought in by bus for the start of the infamous Treason Trial, at which Mandela and others were tried. One man climbed onto the back of the bus to shout encouragement to the inmates.

The ANC leaders' involvement in the five-year Treason Trial process, and their neglect of the day-to-day business of political organization, had the result, too, of creating conditions for the formation of a breakaway group of Africanists. Unhappy about the ANC's multiracialism and the perceived communist grip on the leadership, this group formed the Pan-Africanist Congress (PAC) in 1959 on an exclusively black nationalist platform. As such, the PAC had from its inception more in common with nationalist movements in other parts of decolonizing Africa than did the ANC, loyal to the Freedom Charter's principles, as Mandela would discover. Its finger on the populist pulse, the PAC in March 1960 triggered the anti-pass protests to which the police responded, as will be seen, with the venomous brutality of the Sharpeville massacre.

The demands of his political activity produced dramatic developments, too, in Mandela's personal life. His marriage to Evelyn crumbled, ending in divorce in 1958, and he became smitten with the glamorous young Winnie Madikizela, herself from an eminent Transkei family, and said to be Johannesburg's first black social worker. She was drawn by his chiefly style, he by her charm, good looks, and the glittering image their relationship projected: together they shared a love of dress and fashion that to Mandela compensated for her political naïveté. His letters to her from prison, drenched with images of tropical dancing, delicate touches, and powerful flavors, confirm the widely held impression of friends that the relationship was, throughout, fueled by a strong erotic charge—"electric shocks" in Mandela's phrase. (As late as 1978 he wrote to her from prison: "The mere sight of you, even the thought of you, kindles a thousand fires in me.") Winnie already expressed the headstrong qualities for which she later became famous, and then infamous, yet it was clear she was at this point overawed by Mandela, aware that she was marrying a struggle as much as a man. As with Evelyn, Mandela's expectations of marriage to Winnie were fairly traditional, though he did not discourage her desire to become involved in politics, initially in the women's campaign against carrying passes.

With the turn of the new decade, several African nations won their political independence from the one-time colonial power, Britain. Against this heady background, the PAC and ANC launched separate anti-pass protests, that of the PAC featuring mass arrests at police stations and the ANC's pass burning. On March 21, 1960, in a southern Transvaal town, a crowd of 10,000 surrounded the police station and the panicking police opened fire, killing sixty-nine. This was the dramatic turning point of Sharpeville, which led to the outlawing of the ANC and PAC, the unanimous international condemnation of South Africa, and the declaration of a national state of emergency. In Mandela's view, the parallel PAC and ANC protests had sparked an early revolutionary situation, though he also believed that both organizations had seriously underestimated the ferocity of their Afrikaner opposition.

In the midst of this political storm, Tambo left the country in secret to continue the ANC's struggle abroad, from a London office, and Mandela, imprisoned for five months, was called to give evidence at the Treason Trial. In his first major opportunity for public speaking in years he talked about his different ideological allegiances, to African nationalism, Congress multiracialism, and communism. Thereafter, he wound up his legal practice and condensed the mass movement that had been the ANC around its central "core," as per the M-plan, to enable it to survive underground. Still fired by revolutionary optimism, the ANC organized an All-In African Conference for March 26, 1961, in Pietermaritzburg, Natal, to call for a National Convention of all races to plan a new constitution. A mass protest involving strike action and transport boycotts was called for May 31, when South Africa was due to become a republic.

His most recent banning order having expired, Mandela augmented the hype sparking around his name by appearing at the March conference in a checked three-piece suit, highly polished shoes, and a beard, the last a mark of the radical persona he was cultivating. His speech, which some regarded as lackluster yet which was punctuated with cheers from the audience, would be his last-but-one on a public platform for twenty-nine years. It ended with the cry of *Amandla ngawethu!* (Power is ours!), and gave an important fillip to the Mandela personality cult—as did his clandestine meetings with newspaper editors to explain the ANC's vision. Until his arrest in 1962, Mandela, calling himself David Motsamayi, and more publicly dubbed the Black Pimpernel, lived in hiding and on the run, moving between safe houses in a series of disguises: night watchman, student, agricultural demonstrator, petrol attendant.

In 1961 the Treason Trial finally collapsed with a full acquittal for all. After years of farcical legal posturing on the part of the state, and of skillful legal wrangling by the defense (Victor Berrangé, Bram Fischer, and later Sydney Kentridge), the judges had been unable to establish that the ANC had planned to overthrow the state by violence. Mandela almost immediately disappeared underground in order to organize the planned mass protests against the new apartheid-based republic. He would discover in this process an even greater aptitude for organization and spokesmanship than even he knew he possessed. Given that the ANC's entire leadership was banned, the planned May 31 strike was a relative success though a media failure, the government claiming in the press that it had successfully called off the three-day action on the first day. As in 1952 and 1955, Mandela saw that the state was engaged in systematically closing down virtually every available avenue of nonviolent activism. May 1961 had drawn a line under further possibilities for peaceful resistance.

Despite the then opposition of Chief Luthuli, winner of the 1961 Nobel Peace Prize, Mandela during the second half of that year worked steadily through the arguments for *armed struggle*, as Chapter 4 explores. A July meeting with Indian, white communist, and other allies resolved that Umkhonto we Sizwe (MK, "Spear of the Nation"—the coinage was Mandela's) should be formed as a powerful instrument "that would take the struggle to the heart of white power." Though affiliated to the ANC, Umkhonto was to operate as a separate group, to allow the former to continue as a political organization (though suffering the handicap, inevitably, of leadership neglect). MK would be committed to *sabotage*, not yet outright terrorism or warfare, to keep the way open for reconciliation at a later date.

There was never any doubt that the forceful and militant Mandela would serve as MK commander-in-chief, responsible for setting up the organization and appointing staff. On December 16, 1961, a public holiday to commemorate the Afrikaners' defeat of the Zulus in 1838, the Spear of the Nation launched its first sabotage campaign with a series of successful bomb explosions at government buildings and electric substations in three major cities. By this stage the ANC High Command, in close collaboration with the already long-term underground SACP, was operating out of a secret headquarters, Liliesleaf Farm, situated in the verdant semirural Johannesburg suburb of Rivonia.

On January 10, 1962, Mandela secretly left South Africa in order to attend the Pan-African Freedom Movement for East and Central Africa (PAFMECA) conference in Addis Ababa as the ANC delegate. As well as speaking at the conference—his paper entitled "A Land Ruled by the Gun"—his key purpose was to make contact with other African governments and nationalist groups, and, covertly, seek opportunities for the training of MK cadres. His six months' journey effectively traced a Pan-African map, crisscrossing the continent from east, to north, to west, and north and west again. In Tanzania he debated with Julius Nyerere about the indigenous basis of African socialism. In West Africa (other than Senegal), and at the PAFMECA conference, he experienced hostility on account of the ANC's multiracialism, reflected in his expressed view that Arab Africans were Africans too.

Thereafter, he met Algerian Front de Libération Nationale representatives in Morocco, one of whom, Houari Boumedienne, shared with him the insight that armed liberation movements best succeed when they push toward the negotiation table. In London he talked to Labor and Liberal MPs and paid his respects to Western democracy by visiting Parliament Square (where in 2007 his statue would be erected). In Ethiopia he began a military training program, which was abruptly curtailed, however, when Sisulu recalled him to South Africa. Briefly returning to Johannesburg, Mandela set out almost immediately for Durban, to report to Luthuli and dispel rumors that he had turned Africanist in reaction to Africa-wide preconceptions that the ANC was "communist-dominated."

## Symbol of Justice

At least one—probably more—informers were present at the meetings Mandela held in Natal in late July and early August 1962, still wearing his African battle fatigues. The police were in any case properly tipped off about the date of his return journey to Johannesburg, August 5, 1962. Close to the Natal Midlands town of Howick, they halted his car and he submitted to arrest. He was then held in Johannesburg's Fort Prison, charged with inciting people to a strike and leaving the country without a valid passport. In the trial on October 13, Mandela conducted his own defense, struck by the iconic possibilities he represented as a lawyer-defendant, a "symbol of justice in the court of the oppressor." He opened with an address questioning the legitimacy of a white court to try him. His November 7 plea in mitigation he built into a political testament and the pedestal to his new international reputation, chastising a government that brought the law "into disrepute" in its treatment of peaceful black protest. He was sentenced to five years' imprisonment, the first seven months of which were spent in Pretoria Central Prison, where he met the PAC leader Robert Sobukwe—almost as influential and masterful a leader as Mandela in this period—and the following six weeks on Robben Island.

Mandela was recalled from Robben Island following the July 12, 1963, surprise police raid on Liliesleaf Farm, where most of the key ANC and MK leaders were arrested and a hoard of incriminating documents discovered. Notoriously, these documents included a draft script entitled "Operation Mayibuye" planning a guerrilla invasion of the country, and Mandela's African diary. The prisoners were charged with sabotage and conspiracy, for which the penalty, as for high treason, was death. After the defense team overturned the prosecution's initial sloppy indictment (and the freed accused were immediately re-arrested), the trial proper began on December 3, the state presenting a raft of documentary evidence and 173 witnesses, including Bruno Mtolo, an informer from Durban.

The accused and their lawyers (among them Berrangé, Fischer, Joel Joffe, Arthur Chaskalson) were aware that the cornerstone of their defense was to use the courtroom as a stage on which to present their beliefs. They realized they would have to admit the charge of sabotage, but would—correctly—deny that MK had already embarked on guerrilla war. Instead they would have to explain the turn to *graduated armed resistance*, emphasizing that war was reserved as a last resort if all else failed. Mandela in particular decided to forfeit the debating forum provided by the witness box, to present directly from the dock a statement of his views concerning militancy and democracy. This both played upon, and substantially reinforced, the heroic image his time underground had created. It was Sisulu who spent five days under cross-examination, resolutely sticking to the line that Operation Mayibuye (or Come Back) had been a proposal only.

. . . . .

"I have dedicated myself to this struggle of the African people. I have fought against White domination, and I have fought against Black domination. I have cherished the ideal of a democratic and free society in which all persons live together in harmony and with equal opportunities. It is an ideal which I hope to live for and to achieve. But, if needs be, it is an ideal for which I am prepared to die."

*Nelson Mandela, Conclusion to Rivonia Trial Statement to the Court (1964)*

. . . . .

In his carefully modulated statement on April 20, 1964, oscillating between personal history and political vision, Mandela as in 1962 invoked the influence upon his political beliefs of his African background, in particular of the to-him-egalitarian structures of precolonial African society. He drew attention to the government's intransigence: despite peaceful protest, the "rights of Africans [had become] less instead of becoming greater." Throughout, he was concerned to underline the ANC's and even MK's distance from the SACP, though he did not disavow that connections between the groups existed, on the grounds of common cause and expediency. Socialist redistribution, he said, was to be recommended to allow "our people" to "catch up" with the advanced nations. He declared himself an admirer of the Westminster parliamentary system. He rounded off what is still counted as his most powerful speech with the poised, now-famous statement abjuring racial exclusivity, causing a sigh of acclaim to sweep through the court—and then swiftly to ripple around the world via full-text reports in the international news media.

The state's sentence was eventually pronounced on June 12, 1964. To demonstrate the firmness of their beliefs, the accused decided not to appeal if a death sentence were passed. Should this be the case Mandela did, however, prepare a few lines of response. Here he reiterated the resolute spirit of the speech from the dock, commemorated the sacrifice of those who demanded their rights, whose forces were growing, and expressed the hope of meeting his death "like a man." In the event, the Rivonia sentence was life imprisonment for eight of the nine accused, Judge Quartus de Wet having accepted that Operation Mayibuye had not progressed beyond the planning stage. Late that night, the Rivonia prisoners were taken by air to Robben Island Maximum Security Prison.

# THREE

## Growth of a National Icon:
## Later Years

●

NELSON MANDELA AND THE OTHER RIVONIA PRISONERS—his friend Sisulu; the young, politically astute Kathrada; Govan Mbeki, the eldest and a Marxist; quiet Raymond Mhlaba; and the two trade unionists, Andrew Mlangeni and Elias Motsoaledi—arrived on Robben Island for their at-that-point-indefinite sojourn on a cold June 13. The white prisoner Dennis Goldberg continued to be held in Pretoria. Although handcuffed, Mandela alone had not been manacled en route and rightly suspected that this (along with later privileges such as the permission to continue his University of London LL.B. studies), had to do with his Thembu aristocratic connections, accentuated by his new international reputation.

**"Free Mandela"** was the rallying motto, if not the mantra, for the anti-apartheid movement throughout Mandela's long imprisonment, from November of 1962 to February of 1990. In this photograph, taken in 1965, a young man removes graffiti from a wall of King's College Chapel in Cambridge, England.

Since Mandela's first visit, Robben Island had been redesigned to accommodate more long-term political prisoners. A strict, racially tagged warder-prisoner hierarchy existed within which the all-Afrikaans white warders were distinguished by their rural or working-class origins, and poor level of education (certainly vis-à-vis the inmates). Mandela's cell in the isolation section, or Section B, was about eight and a half by seven and a half feet square and lit day and night with a forty-watt bulb. The thirty Section B prisoners were cut off from newspapers, radio, and all other channels to the outside world. They were allowed very few visits and two letters a year from close relatives, which were usually heavily censored. At first news came mainly through the conduit that new prisoners provided merely by their presence: in 1965 these included Laloo Chiba and Mac Maharaj, successors to Mandela in the MK High Command.

From the perspective of mainland South Africa, the prisoners had been rendered in every way nonpersons, inhabitants of an otherworldly "arena" (Mandela's image), in which they and their captors formed the sole audience to their actions. The reflective atmosphere, intellectual achievements, and moral symbolism that mark Mandela's prison period are elaborated in Chapter 7. The narrative here concentrates on the chronological unfolding of the quarter-century-plus of his incarcerated life, a trajectory leading him through the final decades of apartheid, into the glare of national and international acclaim.

## In the Island Prison

Soon after the prisoners' arrival on the island, Mandela protested over the racist distinction that Africans, in contrast with Indian and Colored prisoners, were made to wear khaki shorts, rather than long trousers. For the Johannesburg gentleman such petty discrimination in the matter of clothes was doubly unacceptable, a two-pronged affront to personal dignity. Over the years he would motivate other typically "nonviolent" protests at the injustices of the prison system: walking slowly in response to the command to move faster; refusing to call any warder *baas* (master). He joined with and led the other prisoners—all hyperpoliticized men—in observing a largely unspoken but *regulated social contract* that knit them together as a community. For the one-time firebrand, even his few outbursts of emotion were now calculated, almost choreographed. For example, when in 1970 he complained to the Commissioner of Prisons about warder assaults, it was on the basis of the coolly presented argument that the prison system preserve the law and order it claimed it stood for.

· · · · ·

Nelson Mandela.

> Crime—sabotage.

> Sentence—life plus five years.

>> *The wording of Mandela's prison identity card at the Rivonia Trial (1964)*

· · · · ·

From the beginning, his fellow inmates looked to Mandela as a moral authority and model of behavior: this was the leader who had coped with flair and competence during his time underground. He, together with the three others who had served on the ANC national executive, Sisulu, Mbeki, and Mhlaba, all Xhosa-speaking, formed a prisoner ruling body, the "High Organ." There were, however, strong differences and some-times rifts within this body, even when its membership was widened. Splits emerged especially between the more rigorous Marxists like Mbeki, and more inclusive, mass-support African nationalists such as Mandela, who advocated political and economic reform over outright revolution in order to achieve their primary goal—the end of racial oppression.

Early on, Mandela worked out means of ameliorating the Section B situation from within, and not only through strategically conforming to its (imposed and self-imposed) rules. In particular, noticing from close observation that the warders were not uniformly depraved as characters, he perceived that in individual cases it might be possible to appeal man-to-man to what he saw as their underlying human capacity for change. In his view, the prison system rewarded brutes for their brutish behavior, whereas a different approach might produce a modified response.

Once study privileges were granted, Mandela elected to learn Afrikaans in order to facilitate this process. Afrikaans was after all the language of many black South Africans—as he boldly asserted even at the time of the Soweto protests against the use of Afrikaans in black schools. He suspected that African perceptions of Afrikaners linked to "English" prejudices dating from the time of the Boer War, and was, by contrast, impressed at Afrikaner claims to belong to Africa. Afrikaners, he perceived, shared with black Africans a history of guerrilla-led resistance against imperial exploitation. He kept in mind examples of dissident Afrikaners, such as his friend the communist lawyer Bram Fischer, and the outspoken writers Breyten Breytenbach and André Brink. As he presciently said in one of his important 1976 prison essays about unity within the freedom struggle:

> We ought to speak directly to the Afrikaner and fully explain our
> position. Honest men are to be found on both sides of the color line
> and the Afrikaner is no exception. . . . [even if] this country [is]

reduced to ashes it will still be necessary for us to sit down together and talk about the problems of reconstruction—the black man and the white, the African and the Afrikaner.

This perception, that dialogue could be forged between the two polarized groups on the basis of their shared feelings of *nationalist loyalty* to the country, and that *Afrikaner support* was a prerequisite for reconstruction, represents one of the most important intellectual breakthroughs Mandela experienced on Robben Island.

For their part, the warders came in time to see that they relied on Mandela's cooperation in order to deal constructively with the political prisoner community. In this simple but powerful perception of mutual, interpersonal understanding, the ground for the 1990s *negotiation process* was effectively laid down. The young warders' political education by prisoners was, wrote Neville Alexander, one of "the great human events" on the island. Even the rebellious Soweto generation who arrived from 1977 was eventually inducted into the older men's principle that the authorities should be dealt with in a controlled, rational manner. Negotiation with the enemy, said Sisulu, need not equate with selling out.

From 1965, the prisoners were set to work in the island's glittering white lime quarry. Sunday religious services alone, including by a Cape Town imam, represented a break from this "monotonous routine" of "uncreative work," as Mandela's autobiography describes it. Despite complaints, the severe regimen reached a crisis point in 1971 under commanding officer Colonel Piet Badenhorst. At this tenth anniversary of the ANC's last political campaign, numbers of Section B prisoners, not including Mandela, were terrifyingly assaulted in their cells. He led a delegation to protest to the prison authorities, and thereafter conditions incrementally improved.

Needless to say, there were few "public" events to mark Mandela's Robben Island years, though in mainland South Africa the 1970s and 1980s brought tumultuous mass protests, savage police and military clampdowns, and, ultimately, dramatic political change. In 1964 there were two visits to the prisoners from journalists. On the second occasion of these the famous, and only official, island pictures of Nelson and his fellow inmates were taken, in which he is pictured talking to Walter Sisulu and sewing a jersey, rather than breaking stones, his usual activity. In later years there would also be Red Cross visits, drop-ins by British politicians like Denis Healey, and eight visits from the indomitable Progressive Party MP Helen Suzman, in addition to those from government politicians. Each time Mandela took the opportunity to lodge complaints about the degrading uniform, poor food, and warder assaults, and sometimes obtained results. In 1967 he fought for a second, once-again-successful time to keep his name on the Transvaal Law Society's roll.

Newspapers and magazines—filched, smuggled, obtained as study materials—represented a crucial lifeline, though one that prisoners could not, until the 1980s, depend upon. There was intermittent, necessarily one-way contact with the ANC abroad via released prisoners, and occasional exchanges of coded messages, as with Oliver Tambo. Although Mandela was by now widely regarded as the *de facto* ANC leader, Acting President Tambo was officially confirmed in his role in 1977. Mandela, a party man to the bone, never ceased to support his modest and retiring friend as his leader. SACP member Joe Slovo, meanwhile, had been appointed MK commander (the ANC having officially admitted all races at its 1969 Morogoro conference). There were two or three plans to spring Mandela from the island, but these were never thoroughgoing.

. . . . .

"My current circumstances give me advantages my compatriots outside jail rarely have. Here the past literally rushes to memory and there
is plenty of time for reflection. One is able to stand back and look at
the entire movement from a distance, and the bitter lessons of prison
life force one to go all out to win the cooperation of all fellow prisoners, to learn how to see problems from the point of view of others
as well, and to work smoothly with other schools of thought in the
movement. Thrown together by the fates we have no choice but to
forget our differences in the face of crisis, talk to one another mainly
about our background, hopes, and aspirations, our organizations and
the kaleidoscope of experiences in the field of struggle."

*Nelson Mandela, "National Liberation" (1976)*

. . . . .

The early 1970s saw marked improvements in prison conditions: hot
water, permission to play tennis, and relief from quarry work in the form
of seaweed collection along the island's rocky shores. By 1975, Mandela
was classed as an "A" group prisoner, allowing him three letters and two
noncontact visits a month. At the time of his sixtieth birthday in 1978,
probably unbeknownst to him, the ANC alongside the Anti-Apartheid
Movement based in London, established the Free Mandela campaign as
a central strategic plank upon which to mobilize across a broader political spectrum. This represented a major departure from the tradition of
asserting collective leadership only. The 1978 decision became the germ
of an extraordinarily successful global campaign—movement is the more
accurate term—promoting and to some extent sanitizing the one-time
radical's reputation as a redemptive national hero. This campaign he

himself later tactically manipulated to the advantage of party and policy, yet also rhetorically overrode, as in his consistent appeal to the collective ("we are happy"). His seventieth birthday party in 1988, a rock concert held at Wembley stadium in London, was broadcast to two hundred million viewers worldwide. It is difficult to imagine the success of Mandela's post-1990 image as the long-suffering, even Christ-like, savior of a nonracial South Africa without the essential undergirding that these mass media campaigns provided across his decades of political obscurity on Robben Island.

The most important prisoner activity of all was study: this constituted the pioneering, grassroots "University of Robben Island," in Unity Movement Neville Alexander's felicitous phrase; "a center of learning" in Mandela's. The self-discipline of study fitted the internal contract of disciplined behavior and self-governance that the inmates tacitly attempted to follow. At first, quarry sessions were used for "Socratic" question-and-answer discussions: those who already had a tertiary education taught those who were working toward a certificate or degree. Later teaching was more organized, and included larger group discussion, and, of course, the independent study provided by early evening confinement to the cells. Many islanders used the correspondence courses offered by the University of South Africa, the country's main long-distance-learning institution. Smuggled copies of important yet inaccessible books, especially Marxist texts, written out verbatim through the night in foolscap notepads, were distributed through the prison sections.

By the late 1970s, Mandela's days were filled top-to-bottom with group discussion (prisoner-to-warder, interorganizational, legal advice sessions), as well as gardening in the prison compound, and wide-ranging reading. He was now addressed using his clan name or honorific Madiba. During these years he read realist fiction, Tolstoy, Steinbeck, and Gordimer, much political biography, including of Churchill and Kennedy, the Koran in English translation, the historian Eddie Roux, Samir Amin on neocolonialism, and nineteenth-century English poetry. His bookshelves featured such titles as *Elements of Price Theory*, Oliver and Fage's *Short History of Africa*, Hal Fisher's *A History of Europe*, and *The New English Bible*. Although he missed the Xhosa poetry that had as a student imbued in him a "sense of destiny," he worked his way through Afrikaans literature, convinced that this would give further insight into this people's patriotic resilience of spirit. Despite such seemingly liberal reading opportunities, he was between 1977 and 1981 forbidden from studying toward his LL.B.—a punishment imposed when his secret autobiography was discovered.

## Winnie Madikizela-Mandela

Throughout Mandela's years in prison, Winnie Mandela represented an important source of comfort, solace, and hope—"a real brick," said her husband. She managed, despite the censored letters, to keep open a thin but vital line of connection with political developments in the country. Yet her strictly noncontact visits were always few and far between. In the end this would be the greatest pain of prison life for Mandela: the imposed distance from his adored wife and children, a distance which produced the mesh of cool control that would eventually enwrap virtually his entire public personality. In 1968 his mother died, not long after her first and only island visit. In 1969 there was a second blow, the death in a car crash of his eldest son, Thembi, with whom he had had no contact since 1962. In both cases, he was not given permission to attend the funerals and grieved mostly in silence and alone.

**Mandela's marriage to**
Winnie Madikizela (b. 1936)
lasted for nearly thirty-four years.
This photograph, taken in 1962,
conveys the couple's playful
intimacy, the memory of which
sustained Mandela during his
long years in prison.

As for Winnie, for the duration of her husband's time in prison she operated under relentless pressure, suffering almost constant police surveillance, harassment, and banishment. She lost her prestigious job as a social worker for the petty reason of having failed to report to the Cape Town police on her first trip to the island. A different kind of pressure was exerted by the exigencies of the African nationalist struggle. Despite her relative youth and inexperience, she was placed in the position of having, as she said, to "deputize" for the imprisoned or exiled ANC High Command (though she was never admitted to its inner enclaves as an officeholder). Yet her feisty articulateness and irrepressible attitude of defiance helped her cope. Especially during her years of banishment to the small Free State town of Brandfort (1977–84), she became a key spokesperson for the anti-apartheid cause and an important political player in her own right.

To speak of Winnie Madikizela-Mandela with the benefit of hindsight demands some mention of her darker, less feisty side. It is important to address the situation directly, as it has often been hedged about with deliberate obfuscation, including on Mandela's part. For one so self-disciplined and apparently incorruptible, his bedazzlement over Winnie produced in his personal life a major moral blind spot. On Robben Island and subsequently, he always sought to hold her in high regard as a wife and comrade, despite grim evidence to the contrary. As he wrote in a 1970 letter, he believed that the cruelty of the treatment she had suffered at the hands of the police considerably outweighed his. This observation, while it cannot be taken as a justification of her behavior, does however carry explicatory weight.

Comparing her early career as "mother" of the struggle with later developments, it is evident that aspects of Winnie Mandela's consistently inhumane treatment by the South African police, including lengthy interrogation and shock-separations from her children, exacted serious psychological—and ethical—damage. Her May 1969 to September 1970 detention under the Terrorism Act was particularly difficult, causing Mandela deep anxiety. She always managed to couch her "brutalization" (her own word) in a fiercely African nationalist, anti-Boer rhetoric: yet in this there was a certain truth. Many of her sinister acts, including her homophobic vendettas against young "informers," were motivated by a paranoid nationalism, in that she targeted those—whites and Indians especially, but also Africans—she deemed to have behaved in un-African (including so-called effeminate) ways.

In the 1980s and subsequently Winnie Mandela became implicated in forms of organized violence the illegality of which was at first difficult to establish because of the untrustworthiness of the township police under apartheid. Her "Football Club" of bodyguards was involved in brutal disturbances, eventually landing themselves in a complicated assault and murder case involving the child "Stompie" Seipei, in which fingers were pointed at the Club's powerful mentor. As novelist Njabulo Ndebele later wrote, Winnie, drunk on power, acted at this point as if she "owned" the struggle. When in the early 1990s she served as an ANC welfare officer, and in 1995–6 as Deputy Minister of Arts, Culture, Science, and Technology, she was on several occasions accused of corruption, for which she consistently refused to acknowledge responsibility. Her trial in early 1991 confirmed her conviction for kidnapping in the Football Club incident, but the Truth and Reconciliation Commission found she was more of an accessory to assault and murder than even the 1991 judgment had allowed.

Driven by loyalty, deep feeling, guilt, and a measure of patriarchal responsibility, Mandela stubbornly proclaimed his wife's innocence long after her credibility had been fatally undermined. Yet even he was eventually persuaded to concede that she had done his family's good reputation harm. In 1992 he grimly announced his separation from Winnie and spoke of his sense of extreme isolation. Their divorce was finalized in 1996.

## Toward the End of Apartheid

Two years into Mandela's period of incarceration, the one-time Afrikaner fascist sympathizer B. J. Vorster replaced the assassinated prime minister H. F. Verwoerd without significant change in apartheid ideology or policy. Such hope as eventually emerged for the underground opposition came from an external source, the independence in 1974 of the former Portuguese colonies of Angola and Mozambique, a clear sign that the groundswell of the African liberation struggle was at last moving southward. The Robben Island prisoners rightly adjudged that these frontline states might provide an essential springboard for MK incursions, but did not bargain for the South African government's cynical ability to make deals with its neighbors, most notably with Mozambique in 1984. They also did not fully foresee the extent to which the southern African shift toward independence, and concomitant growing ideas of black self-awareness, were to inspirit the voteless masses within the country itself.

In contrast with the demoralized post-1964 period, the turn of the 1960s saw the reemergence of black political organization in the form of the Black Consciousness movement (BCM) under the charismatic Steve Biko, and the rise of a confident, structured trade union movement in the country's burgeoning industrialized areas. Inspired by the idea that the *black man* should speak for himself, not be spoken for (the generic pronoun was unquestioned), which was drawn from both African-American movements of self-determination and Frantz Fanon's work, Biko in 1968 formed the all-black South African Students' Organization, the kernel of BC. With strong bases in Natal and the Eastern Cape, the BCM was particularly concerned to address the great quag of political apathy and abjection to which South Africa's black population had been reduced. It used a range of well-tried tactics, not unlike those deployed some decades before by the ANC—meetings, rallies, marches, politicized trials, boycotts. Yet its central emphasis on racial exclusivity and self-determination for black Africans departed from and questioned the Congress's multiracial agenda. Depending on the observer's vantage point, this either made the ANC seem out of touch, or the BCM appear "embryonic and clannish," to cite Mandela's critical if defensive assessment in a second 1976 prison essay, "Whither the Black Consciousness Movement?"

The BCM's significant contribution was to infuse those whose experience under apartheid left them feeling worthless with a sense of pride: that belief in self that Mandela for one never lost. The powerless were empowered with sufficient anger to defy their oppressors when armed only with stones—as was starkly demonstrated on June 16, 1976, and in subsequent weeks when schoolchildren first in Soweto and then in the Cape protested at Afrikaans being their compulsory medium of instruction. As at Sharpeville, the police fired upon the crowds of unarmed marchers. By the end of the year, over 650 had lost their lives, and many more had been wounded. Hundreds left the country to seek guerrilla training abroad.

In spite of—or indeed perhaps because of—the fact that the ANC had not anticipated the action, Mandela in "We Shall Crush Apartheid," a statement smuggled out of Robben Island, was quick to identify with the Soweto students' action. It was a typically shrewd maneuver, which counterbalanced the High Command's shock at the intense anarchic militancy of the BCM-inspired protesters who eventually arrived on the island as political prisoners, having been captured as insurgents. Numbers of them had been tortured before being tried. As reflected in "Whither the Black Consciousness Movement?," the ANC leaders from henceforth took determined steps to persuade BCM men like "Terror" Lekota of the wisdom of racial openness, and of the pragmatic advantages of joining forces with other oppositional groups, including the SACP.

All shades of opinion were in their different ways profoundly shaken by the news in September 1977 of Steve Biko's death in detention, and the banning of eighteen BC individuals and groups. Although the BCM emphasis on racial identity had for a time appeared to its critics

**Soweto, an urban area in Johannesburg,** was the scene of a series of bloody clashes between South African youth and the police on June 16, 1976. In the event now known as the Soweto uprising, students rebelled against a decree from the government that would have required their classes in mathematics, arithmetic, and social studies to be conducted in Afrikaans.

to cooperate with state forms of segregation, it was now clear that Black Consciousness nationalism had been declared as much of a threat to apartheid as either communism or the Freedom Charter. The ANC in exile, under Tambo, shifted its military emphasis from discrete incursions to a people's war based on locally planned operations, though the focus was still on bringing all allies under its "revolutionary umbrella." For Mandela, too, violence remained only one tool among others for forcing the government to negotiate.

Not long after the finger-wagging P. W. Botha became prime minister in 1978, ANC bombs were successfully exploded at three separate state installations. The government counterattacked with cross-border strikes into Mozambique and military involvement against Cuban forces in Angola. A cycle of ever-widening mass protest and state reaction dictated the order of the day up till 1990. With South Africa happy to use its long-standing anticommunist crusade in the service of defending apartheid (and with Mandela still branded an "arch-Marxist"), the subcontinent was rapidly turning into one of the major endgames of the Cold War.

Cold War divisions were thrust even upon the longest-serving prisoners on Robben Island. In 1982, without warning, Mandela, Sisulu, Mhlaba, and Mlangeni were taken away to the mainland Cape Town prison of Pollsmoor, an institution for common-law prisoners, splitting them off from prominent Marxists on the island like Mbeki and Kathrada (who, however, was to join the group some months later). This was an important development, presaging that the government might have a different view of Mandela's future role than their public intransigence suggested. Conditions in the prisoners' top-floor rooms in Pollsmoor were noticeably more comfortable than before (they had television for the first time), yet Mandela missed the island's "natural splendors" and the lively company of the other inmates. As compensation, he exploited the new freedoms of his position by embarking on a program of letter-writing, reestablishing chains of contact that had lain dormant for years, and forging links with newspaper men and, in particular, the government minister Kobie Coetsee. Further comfort was drawn from beginning a new garden, as will be seen.

In 1983 Botha set in place a segregated "tricameral parliament" including Indians and Coloreds alongside whites, but excluding blacks, who were believed to enjoy representation in the so-called independent black homelands. In response, the forces of opposition in the country formed a loose coalition of activist groups, the United Democratic Front.

The UDF, though arguably inspired by the activist legacies of the ANC, was, however, like the BCM, independently constituted. Despite detentions and assassinations, the UDF was to prove adaptive and resilient in mounting resistance to the government for several years, until its banning in February 1988. Its emergence was followed by the formation in 1987 of the well-organized Congress of South African Trade Unions, while church leaders under Archbishop Tutu became ever more passionate in their condemnation of apartheid. In February 1989, at a time of several successful strikes, the Mass Democratic Movement rose hydralike in the place of the banned UDF.

Faced with this volatile situation, in which resistance was mounting across an ever-broader terrain, including internationally, Mandela could not but chafe against his prison-enforced isolation. He strongly felt he had insights gleaned over decades to contribute to finding a solution to the gathering crisis. In January 1985, Tambo called for South Africa to be "rendered ungovernable," a move which Mandela, Sisulu, and the others supported though with reservations. In the same month Botha offered Mandela his freedom, conditional upon a rejection of violence. (Mandela's state-approved rival, the antisocialist Zulu nationalist Chief Mangosuthu Buthelezi, was among those who said it would be ill-advised to let him unconditionally walk free.) Mandela wrote a careful response to Botha's offer, read by his daughter Zindzi at a Soweto mass meeting on February 10, 1985. He reiterated his support for the leadership in exile, as if to quash in advance any suggestion that he might act unilaterally, and ended by powerfully announcing that his freedom could not be negotiated separately from that of his people.

Meanwhile, in the townships, violence escalated in the form of street battles, militant funeral marches, rent-boycott protests, and intracommunity "necklacing" (in which alleged collaborators were garlanded with burning tires). A dense pall of stirred-up dust and tear gas hung permanently over the township streets. On July 20, 1985, Botha declared a state of emergency and Western banks at last threatened to stop bankrolling the South African state, which however showed no willingness to make terms. In September, the US agreed to kick-start the process of imposing sanctions on the country.

## The Negotiating Concept

Signs that the government at least wanted Mandela alive and well emerged around the time of his prostate operation in December 1985, when he was personally visited by the Minister of Justice, Kobie Coetsee, and allowed to convalesce in a separate cell within Pollsmoor prison. It was at this point that, as on his departure from the Island, a keen awareness of the need to seize the historical initiative came to Mandela. He saw—or at least it appears he saw—that if he now stepped forward, he might author a fundamental turn in his country's fortunes. It was a sensitive decision; a precarious, knife-edge moment. To act independently was to go against the ANC's tradition of collective leadership, and its current thinking on rolling revolution and people's war. Not to act meant the country plunging further into its present "dark night of oppression," divided into separate camps, with no prospect of military victory on either side. He asked his Pollsmoor colleagues not to protest at the situation of divide-and-rule to which they were now subjected. For the first time in his ANC career, Mandela decided to go it alone: as for any herd-boy, "there are times when a leader must move out ahead of the flock."

His decision at this crucial juncture, offering himself as sole temporary leader (though contacting Tambo for his approval), would prove incisive not only for the ANC, but for his reputation, something of which he was not unaware. To the 1986 Commonwealth Eminent Persons Group, formed to map a route toward peace through dialogue, he appeared to exude authority. Yet his situation was often precarious, even dangerous. He was staking his good political name on the new initiative, and this involved him in talks intercalating with other talks in distant capitals, of which he did not have a full picture. There would be rumors, seemingly well founded, that he was selling out, colluding with the enemy against his own people. Ultimately, however, his conviction of what was politically necessary, and his faith in his ability to "master" or author his country's fate, outweighed his and his colleagues' doubts. After years of enforced waiting Mandela let himself emerge as South Africa's redeeming leader, and in this capacity came forward as one of the preeminent players in the history of twentieth-century anti-imperialism.

· · · · ·

"If this breakfast will kill me then today I am prepared to die."

*James Gregory, quoting Mandela's comment on sitting down to a high-cholesterol breakfast while convalescing, in* Goodbye Bafana *(1995)*

Punning on his own speech from the dock in 1985, Mandela uses the universal emollient of humor, even with his captors.

· · · · ·

Although in mid-1986 the Commonwealth Eminent Persons Group initiative was conclusively negated by South Africa's military attacks on frontline states with ANC bases, the group had however helped to plant an important seed with Mandela. He called it the *negotiating concept*, the idea of forcing principle through dialogue; the careful balancing of undertakings and concessions in order to lay a pathway toward a democratic dispensation. Even as the state of emergency in the country was reimposed, and full-scale civil war seemed imminent, Mandela during an audience with Coetsee asked to see President Botha and Foreign Minister Pik Botha. This was followed up by a second visit from Coetsee in 1987, against a background in which ANC leaders abroad, too, were beginning to have contact with Afrikaner businessmen, politicians, and activists.

Pretoria now put together a team of four, including Coetsee and Niël Barnard, head of National Intelligence, to pursue a way forward with Mandela. He for his part continued to uphold three conditions for further negotiation: a refusal to lay down arms until such time as the ANC gained political power; acceptance of the SACP as the ANC's long-standing fellow traveler; and admission of the principle of majority rule. In 1988 Mandela's ill health, a case of incipient tuberculosis, again added urgency to the still-tentative engagement. At the end of the year, to ensure his continuing separation, the state's key interlocutor was moved to a warder's house at Victor Verster prison in the winelands town Paarl, of which he was permitted sole use.

Mandela saw that the nationalist government was now unreservedly setting him up for a key role in, as he said, the "debate for a new South Africa." He was also acutely aware that determination and tactical wariness would continue to serve as his best weapons against, on the one hand, their attempts to isolate him, and, on the other, the ANC's mistrust (especially at the concession of weakness that negotiation implied). Always a public proponent of liberal democracy, he was falling back per force on a more traditional, patrimonial style of decision taking that recalled the chiefly deliberations he had observed as a youth.

He found himself adept at the skills that the leader-led negotiation process required: the patient restatement of countervailing objectives always informed by a sense of mutual obligation and shared duty (in particular, duty to future generations). At heart, the situation involved the dogmatic, formal citation of conflict in order pragmatically to broker peace. Although widespread suspicion remained, Mandela's assured patrician style is generally considered to have calmed nerves on both sides of the apartheid divide.

In January 1989, the "Old Crocodile" P. W. Botha suffered a stroke, Tambo for his part succumbing to the same affliction only six months later. Botha was replaced as leader of the National Party by F. W. de Klerk, a cautious leader who held the belief that apartheid might work as a means of granting self-determination to the various "nations" that constituted South Africa. Unlike P. W. Botha, however, he was more open to pragmatic deal-making, especially in view of the 1989 crumbling of the Soviet bloc, of which he took careful note. The courtesy call between Mandela and a physically and politically weakened Botha finally took place on July 4, 1989 (six weeks before the latter's final resignation), marked by elaborate gestures of respect on both sides. At the time of Botha's death in October 2006, Mandela reiterated his appreciation for his counterpart's politeness and level dealing, though at the time Botha had turned a deaf ear to Mandela's primary request, for the release of the Rivonia prisoners. In August 1989, the ANC's Harare Declaration laid down the freeing of all political prisoners, the removal of troops from the townships, and the organization's unbanning as conditions for the suspension of the armed struggle.

At the end of that year, Mandela embarked on the first of series of meetings with de Klerk, in which the latter was like his predecessor impressed at the older man's style and knowledge of Afrikaner resistance history. The prospect of his release was coming into focus, though the condition for his agreement was the unbanning of the ANC. Even at this stage, however (and rightly as it turned out), Mandela expressed concern that the government might be continuing apartheid oppression by other means (through what later became known as a Third Force operating within the homelands, and fomenting black-on-black violence). Inkatha under Chief Buthelezi was increasingly operating as a paramilitary force, drawing support from within the Pretoria state apparatus. Mandela would always suspect de Klerk of complicity in this activity, whereas de Klerk, equally motivated by a sense of his importance as a leader, at the same time grew circumspect about Mandela's volatility in his relations with him.

## Birth of an Icon

On February 2, 1990, de Klerk made a significant speech in which, it seemed in one fell swoop, he reversed apartheid policy of the past three decades, and agreed to release the ANC leader-in-the-wings unconditionally. Mandela himself remained calm during this momentous time, concentrated less on the big picture than on the small details of his walk into freedom (that it should be from his prison, alongside Winnie; that he should on the same day give a straightforward ANC policy speech, without rhetorical flourishes).

The Sunday following, a warm February 11, Mandela walked out of Victor Verster "hand in hand" with Winnie, as heralded in Hugh Masekela's well-known song, wearing a characteristically sober suit, his fist raised in the classic ANC salute. Millions across the world, inspired by the stark polarities of the anti-apartheid cause, caught up in the Free Mandela campaign's hype, curious to see the world's longest-serving,

**By the time Mandela was finally released** from prison on February 11, 1990, he had become the world's longest-serving political prisoner as well as its most famous. This photograph shows Mandela, accompanied by his then-wife, Winnie, leaving Victor Verster Prison, where he had spent the last three years of his incarceration.

long-invisible political prisoner, waited in expectation for hours to witness the birth of this new resistance icon.

Despite the disappointment many felt at his formulaic speech from Cape Town city hall expressing his determination to progress the fight for freedom on every front, the newly released leader soon glowed in a softer, more reassuring light. In meeting after meeting, whether high level or low profile, he refused bitterness, praised the integrity of his opponents, acted in deliberately self-effacing ways, talked about talks, and deferred always to "the people's" will. The catalyst of the democratic future had been released back into his "beloved country," as he patriotically called it, and was setting out to render it more worthy of loving than before.

Mandela's major political-ethical standpoints in the 1990s and subsequently are charted in the final chapters of this book. This chapter will close with an overview of the developments that marked his ascent to the presidency, his five years in government, and involvements since.

## Building Freedom

The months following Mandela's release were occupied with a demanding schedule of meetings with well-wishers and adoring crowds around the world, in Zimbabwe and Algeria, in Zambia and Sweden, in London and the United States. For Mandela, however, it was a priority to thank the ANC's many long-standing supporters (including Gadhafi and Castro), and solicit their continuing backing for sanctions—until such time as apartheid be wholly dismantled.

Another priority was to reconnect with ANC comrades in exile, and to attempt, though with a singular lack of success, to dissuade factions in Johannesburg and KwaZulu-Natal, the Inkatha stronghold, from brutally waging war upon one another. It appeared that a hidden force in the South African security establishment was indeed siphoning funds and arms to Inkatha in order to undermine the ANC. Incensed, Mandela considered resuming the armed struggle, suspended in August 1990. It seemed to him sinister that violence tended to erupt in the run-up to negotiations with the government, as if to poison them (as at Sebokeng in March 1990).

In his family life a different kind of internecine war played itself out, as Winnie pursued the extravagant lifestyle to which she had grown accustomed, and in private cold-shouldered her husband. On both sides, it was clear that the long years of separation had corroded the marriage, as they had Mandela's relations with his daughters, who felt he had been a father to the nation at the expense of being a father to them.

Meetings between the ANC and de Klerk's government began in May 1990, though dogged with suspicion on both sides. The greatest challenge Mandela faced was not merely to forge unity within his organization. During a time of deep conflict, and from an inherently weak position, his task was to convince his comrades, many more radical than he, to stay the course of transition, however onerous. A particularly difficult discussion concerned state nationalization, which he continued until 1993 officially to support, in the face of the apparent global triumph of a post–Cold War neoliberalism. It was an open question as to whether South Africa, already weakened by the protectionist, command economy of the apartheid years, would be able to balance social justice with wealth creation vis-à-vis this global system. He and his government were in the end to make costly settlements with international capitalism, in particular the IMF, in the form of South Africa's Reconstruction and Development Program, later modified into GEAR (Growth, Employment, and Redistribution).

In the face of considerable hostility at the extra-party prestige he had acquired, Mandela in pitched arguments within the ANC had often to stand upon *both* the moral authority he had won across the island years, *and* his patrician status. An unfortunate consequence of this dual positioning was that the authority based on experience and the more traditional status tended to become conflated in his colleagues' minds, which exposed him to charges of authoritarian behavior. He had repeatedly to resort to entreaties of caution: the ANC, he urged, should count not only anticolonial liberation but also stable postcolonial governance among its successes; negotiations themselves formed "a theater of struggle." He continued to draw upon the admonishments of Sisulu, the reflectiveness of

Tambo (who in late 1990 stood down as ANC president), and Slovo's remarkable talent for diplomacy. Aides frequently expressed frustration that he appeared to fritter away his energy exchanging pleasantries with unscrupulous moguls and fawning fans. Yet it was clear that he was motivated throughout by a belief in the power of his own ethical position. He was convinced that, if he consistently projected openness to dialogue and a basic human goodwill, others would follow suit.

In September 1991, after revelations concerning the Third Force had significantly undermined de Klerk and Buthelezi's bargaining positions, a national peace accord was struck. In December of that year the Convention for a Democratic South Africa (CODESA 1) was launched with the objective of working for "sufficient consensus" for an "undivided nation." However, both CODESA 1 and 2 (held in May 1992) were bedeviled by various interruptions, stallings, and stalemates. On the very first day a vicious spat broke out between de Klerk and Mandela, neither of whom yet saw how much they needed one another, and in June 1992 the bloody Boipatong massacre, fomented by the security forces, threatened for a time entirely to scupper negotiations. Mandela once again bent every one of his faculties of brokerage and "credentials of sacrifice" to push his colleagues toward balancing the advantages of negotiation against the strong push toward militant remobilization. The ANC Secretary-General Cyril Ramaphosa, a preeminent broker of the talks, noted his calm "brutality" and "nerves of steel," though he was prone to venting his anger in telephonic tirades to de Klerk. De Klerk for his part skillfully reestablished his legitimacy with white voters by winning a March 1992 referendum backing constitutional change.

In February 1993, nearly nine months on from Boipatong, the negotiating parties announced an in-principle agreement to a Government of National Unity (GNU), to sit for five years, though this was made possible only through the trading of various claims and privileges over majority sizes and power-sharing. Mandela believed that the coalition thus forged would stave off the still-present threat of civil war—one that had previously undermined other newly independent African nations. Two months later he was again compelled by circumstances to stand forward as the war-torn country's lone beacon of statesmanlike steadfastness when the charismatic Communist Party Secretary, Chris Hani, was gunned down by a rightwing assassin. Only two weeks later, Oliver Tambo died after a to some extent unsung career keeping the ANC organized during its years in exile.

Mandela used the credit he gained in the aftermath of Hani's death to push for an election date, despite the fact that he and de Klerk continued at loggerheads, and Buthelezi looked set on separatism. The Zulu leader finally agreed to participate in the democratic process only days before the April 27, 1994, elections, an even tardier participant than the Afrikaner Conservative Party. Yet in November 1993 the transition to democracy was made safe with the agreement of an interim constitution (redrawing the provincial map of the country as a concession to federalists like Buthelezi). As if to seal the process, Mandela and de Klerk were jointly awarded the 1993 Nobel Peace Prize, though they remained mutually abrasive in public, even in Stockholm. While Mandela appeared to resent sharing the prestigious symbolic platform with an Afrikaner counterpart whom he refused to prefer to Botha, South Africa's liberation from white minority rule did not delight de Klerk.

The run-up to the 1994 first democratic elections was as, if not more, bloody than any period in the preceding four years of preparation, yet the election day itself, bathed by a warm autumn sun, was as peaceful as anyone could have hoped. Long queues of people waited patiently everywhere across the country to vote, most for the first time in their lives, creating a profoundly moving tableau for the world media, which culminated in victory for the ANC. It seemed a miracle, a resounding conclusion to a people's long journey, and a spontaneous outburst of support for democracy, yet a huge amount of moral energy had gone into its making, on both sides of the apartheid divide.

· · · · ·

> "A fleeting moment when history became utterly important, inescapable, and compelling. Nelson Mandela became President, and the word 'freedom' took on an almost childlike meaning, so magical was its effect."
>
> *Achmat Dangor, from* Bitter Fruit *(2003)*

· · · · ·

Two weeks later, on May 10, Mandela was inaugurated as South Africa's first democratic President in Pretoria, with Thabo Mbeki and de Klerk as his deputies. The vast international crowd sang both the Afrikaner national anthem "Die Stem," and the ANC freedom hymn, "Nkosi Sikelel' iAfrika," now fused together in a compelling instance of the compromise on which the new GNU was based. "Never, never, and never again," Mandela urged in his inaugural speech, in words that are now often cited as the catchphrase for his entire achievement, "shall it be that this beautiful land will again experience the oppression of one by another . . . Let freedom reign." The southernmost reaches of Africa had at last entered the postcolonial age. In lines that the Irish poet Seamus Heaney wrote for his

*The Cure at Troy* at the time of hearing of Mandela's release, "hope" and "history"—for the moment at least—appeared to rhyme.

A genial, hands-off style of leadership characterized Mandela's five years in office, which began, it is worth remembering, when he was already seventy-six years old. The GNU settled down to its task of coalition government with a certain amount of relaxed bonhomie. In May 1996, however, de Klerk withdrew his party from the government, believing he had a more powerful role to play in opposition. In the international arena, Mandela offered the insights of proven experience in helping to broker peace in countries like Angola and Burundi, and was instrumental in securing the release to a neutral third country of the alleged Lockerbie bombers. His stated intention was to place human rights at the center of foreign policy. He was concerned to encourage South-South partnerships and transnational Indian Ocean Rim linkups, as an expression of which he made sure that South Africa made its mark on the Non-Aligned Movement, from which it had previously been excluded. But his moral authority proved useless to resist the tyrannous rule of Nigerian leader General Sani Abacha, who in November 1995 executed the Ogoni writer-agitator Ken Saro-Wiwa, despite international protests. Nigeria demonstrated the grim limits of a human-rights-driven policy.

On the home front Mandela engaged in vibrant displays of conciliation and bridge-building between communities: wearing captain François Pienaar's No. 6 rugby shirt at the Springboks' 1995 Rugby World Cup victory and taking tea with Betsy Verwoerd, the widow of one of apartheid's architects. In October 1996, South Africa's new constitution, probably one of the most rights-friendly in the world, came before Parliament for ratification. He admonished his own party to greater efficiency but his government struggled to deliver on promises of housing and new jobs in the face of declining business confidence in South Africa and a tough economic climate worldwide. He rapidly found that it would prove as challenging a task to win the peace as it had been to wage the struggle for democracy.

In his personal life, he filled the sociable if sometimes lonely days after his presidential inauguration and later divorce with glitzy meetings with international celebrities from the worlds of show business and pop music. Although these were worlds at a light-year remove from the Pollsmoor cell where he once meditated the unified shape of the new South Africa, they nonetheless allowed him to foster, if within a global dimension, the

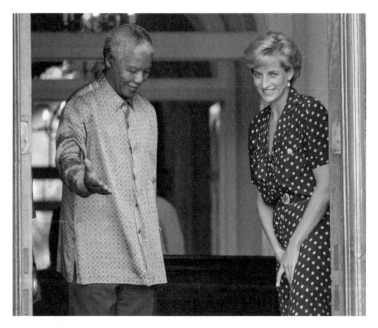

**This strikingly everyday moment** at the door of Mandela's Tuynhuis presidential residence in Cape Town, which drew together two of the twentieth century's most celebrated public figures, was photographed on March 15, 1997.

networks and connections on which his sense of personal identity and authority thrived. Whitney Houston, Whoopi Goldberg, the Spice Girls, Naomi Campbell, Princess Diana—all were extravagantly flattered by Mandela in media acts that involved much mutual image-burnishing, but probably also represented an extension of his delight in urbane performance, even street carnival, something already evident during his early Johannesburg years. Gradually he drew closer to Graça Machel, the widow of Mozambique's first postcolonial leader, Samora Machel, and a freedom fighter in her own right, who supported him both in the dignified management of his personal grief after his divorce, and in the high-profile, often grueling work of leadership politics.

Mandela's most notable achievement was appropriately in the area of ethical conciliation: the need to face up to the wrongs of the past in order to live in greater harmony in the future. His government presided over the launch in 1996 of the Truth and Reconciliation Commission, under the chairmanship of Archbishop Desmond Tutu. Modeled on Chile's 1990 Comisión, the TRC essentially represented a national talking cure through the medium of Christianized public testimony. Perpetrators of crimes of oppression and torture under apartheid were granted quasi-judicial amnesty in exchange for a full confession provided they could demonstrate their acts had been politically motivated. Victims were encouraged to come forward to indict their torturers and so, it was hoped, obtain moral and psychological release from their experience of violation, though importantly with relatively limited prospect of judicial or monetary reparation.

Throughout, till it published its findings in 1998, the TRC remained controversial, with the ANC eventually attempting to block the five-volume final report, against Mandela's advice, for detailing abuses of power committed in its training camps. The Commission's perhaps most important outcome was to have staged a revelatory human drama that offered a historic moment of recognition to the many ordinary victims of apartheid. Although its critics were shocked at the impunity it granted to perpetrators, it provided, through its extensive media coverage, a cathartic process of facing up to the ills of the past. Ultimately, of the more than seven thousand applications for amnesty it received, only 1,146 were granted.

In 1997, after a rip-roaring speech critiquing ANC complacency and careerism, Mandela stepped down as its president. At the June 1999 general election that returned the party to power, he formally handed over to Thabo Mbeki, as he had long promised. His time in government had not delivered as much as it had set out to do, due in part to South Africa's attempts to obey the neoliberal strictures of the global market, yet reforms in respect of township electrification, universal education, and health care were in train. In cities like Johannesburg, black entre-preneurial empowerment was unstoppable; as, too, was a massive crime wave, unhindered by a corrupt, underpaid police force.

Despite near-universal adulation, Mandela had been determined not to remain in office and embody that dreaded cliché, the African presi-dent-for-life. He now took keen interest in building a new house in his childhood village Qunu. The house of course had a garden, redesigned as part of a televised project by a gardening team associated with the BBC. On his eightieth birthday he married Graça Machel, and together with her invested time and energy in a number of children's charities, most notably his own Children's Fund. The enthusiasm and optimism of chil-dren would never fail to chime in with Mandela's commitment to open human interaction, and to creating opportunities for national renewal.

In this same spirit, Mandela began formally to fight to raise HIV/AIDS awareness in late 2001. Complicated denials and cover-ups to do with moralistic reticence and the legacy of racism in Africa had characterized the ANC's handling of the country's pandemic up to this point. Mandela somewhat belatedly waited until he retreated from public office to assume his controversial new role. Yet, once he identified himself with the Treatment Action Campaign, he worked hard to persuade the Mbeki government to make antiretroviral medication available to HIV/AIDS sufferers, one of whom would be his own son, Makgatho, who died in 2005.

In the spirit of historic reconciliation Mandela agreed in 2002 to couple his name to that of the British arch-imperialist yet nation-builder Cecil John Rhodes, to set up the Mandela Rhodes Foundation to foster academic leadership within South African universities. He remained as aware as ever of the nation's need for unifying symbols. His activities were now streamlined into three main strands or "legacy organizations," the Nelson Mandela Foundation, the Nelson Mandela Children's Fund, and the Mandela Rhodes Foundation. He continued his spirited resistance to the US's high-handed behavior on the international stage when in 2003 he sharply criticized the American-British decision to go to war against Saddam Hussein's Iraq. In 2006 Amnesty International, which once had distanced itself from his militancy, awarded him its Ambassador of Conscience award in recognition of his "fearless championing of freedom and justice around the world," including of the rights of HIV/AIDS sufferers.

# FOUR

## Influences and Interactions

●

IN ANY DISCUSSION OF THE HISTORICAL INSPIRATIONS that together created the extraordinary figure of Nelson Mandela, he is often placed in a *relationship of affiliation* with other exemplary anticolonial and antiracism twentieth-century leaders, in particular M. K. Gandhi and Martin Luther King. Then again, as often, Mandela is described as uniquely a product of South Africa's history, shaped by his high-status, rural background, patrician heritage, and long labor against oppression into a warrior for democracy. In this second interpretation, far from standing on the shoulders of other heroes of freedom struggle around the world, Mandela is seen as the primary if not sole author of his story of overcoming.

**With the benefit of hindsight,** certain aspects of Mandela's political practice can be compared with those of Mohandas Gandhi, though Mandela departed from Gandhi's support for nonviolence. In this photograph, taken on October 15, 1990, Mandela sits under a portrait of Gandhi at a banquet in New Delhi hosted by India's then-president Ramaswamy Venkataraman.

What might be the meanings that make up the millennial Madiba (to cite a recent book title)? This chapter will consider Mandela's remarkable life as a meeting point between different cultural and political influences, and traditions of thought and activism—influences that include but exceed patrimonial ideas about obligation derived from his guardian's court, or his sense of self-reliance fostered at school and university. It is of course possible to read his story exclusively under an individualistic heroic heading, as was seen, as the narrative of an independently constituted identity on the road to self-realization through the fight for freedom. Yet such a narrative misses the degree to which the exemplary heroic life, like other lives, is formed in relation to different contingent histories, as an interface between multiple, at times conflicting, discourses and processes of self-definition. Indeed, in view of the prominently collective, eclectic ideological makeup of the ANC, it is unlikely that a man as identified with his movement as was Mandela, could have sprung into the world as a self-made leader of one exclusive political stripe.

Beginning with the literary and political curriculum to which he would have been exposed as a member of a middle-class black elite, the following sections will examine his position in relation to transnational African traditions of political formation and his powerful Gandhist inheritance. The chapter will end by considering his growing susceptibility to arguments in favor of active or armed resistance, as eloquently articulated in 1950s Africa by the Martinique-born, Algeria-based anticolonialist Frantz Fanon—as well as by revolutionary elements within the SACP.

## The Black Elite's Curriculum

Mandela and his generation, including Oliver Tambo and the 1950s *Drum* magazine journalists, were products of a remarkable period of black intellectual flowering in South Africa, emerging from the church schools (St. Peter's, Adam's College, Lovedale, Healdtown), and after 1916 from the college that became the University of Fort Hare. As Mandela was to say years later, these religious institutions were (until the Bantu Education system closed them down) entirely responsible for the "education of blacks," encouraging in them ideals of social duty and a fundamentally modern belief in the autonomous self. Evangelical Christian ideas of salvation through good work and renunciation here entered into their "blood," mixed in with the core concepts of a liberal arts education.

The influence upon Mandela of his training in literary studies and the law at Healdtown and Fort Hare, in an environment that was relatively free of overt racial prejudice, is incalculable. Certainly it reinforced the lessons in moral and communal responsibility introduced at Jongintaba's court. Modeled on the British public school, though with an even greater emphasis on character building through physical rigor, the missionary colleges aimed to create "black Englishmen," instilling in their students the so-called English values of social responsibility and fair play, and the ambition to promote principled, orderly conduct in public life. The highest ideals—necessarily English ideals—and the best expression of character—English character—found their ultimate expression in Shakespeare. Shakespeare and Tennyson were famously taught by Fort Hare's principal Dr. Alexander Kerr with a vividness that made the work—no doubt especially archetypal political plays like *Julius Caesar*—appear immediate and realistic to his students.

Above all, their Christian and liberal humanist education fostered in the African elite a vision of a common humanity transcending social barriers, exemplified in the significance they might find not only in English literature, but also in stories about heroic characters from the British imperial record, like Wellington or Churchill. As Mandela's views on national unity and the possibilities of negotiation after 1990 suggest, the concept of a shared humanness that overrode historical divisions would return to him with force in the seclusion of Robben Island, sustaining his hope in a future free of racism. This vision was predictably again underpinned by the common cultural text that Shakespeare offered to many of the mission-trained political prisoners, not only Mandela. Using Sonny Venkatrathnam's *Collected Works*, prisoners took pleasure in reading and reciting favorite passages, acknowledging to one another that they found in these plays instances of self-awareness, conflict, and triumph over adversity which moved them and with which they could identify.

However, the stirring expression of the drama of humanity was for the student Mandela importantly not confined to Shakespeare and the rhetoric of Churchill. The young man who won the best Xhosa essay prize at Healdtown in 1938 always remained attached to the moving cadences and heart-stopping insights into cultural loss and regeneration of the Xhosa oral tradition, most notably the work of the poet Mqhayi, modeled on praise-songs. Here Mandela found confirmation of his still-parochial patriotic feelings for his Xhosa-speaking Thembu homeland—feelings that he was, however, able to accommodate alongside his knowledge of British history and culture, though not always without a struggle.

Around the same time as Mandela arrived at Fort Hare, the leading Zulu writer B. W. Vilakazi in his poem "Higher Education" memorably spoke of how the "white man's books" and black praise-songs quarreled in his mind. It was a quarrel that was resolvable only if Africans were regarded as much as a part of humanity as whites, a view that Mandela did not hold in doubt but that apartheid of course directly refuted. Yet literature with its insights into the passions and conflicts which moved all societies, at the same time offered pathways to think through such quarrels. As Mandela appears to have found when reading Afrikaans poetry or Nadine Gordimer's *Burger's Daughter* in prison, or when performing Sophocles with fellow inmates, the point where different literatures converged lay in their insights into human subjectivity. Unlike in law books or historical studies, in novels and drama it was possible to see how the personal self sheared away from the politician's agenda.

The canon of first Fabian and nationalist, and then Marxist thought that Mandela worked through in Johannesburg in the 1940s did not necessarily undermine the tenets of his college training, though it did slough away his never-robust Christian faith in favor of a more expansive secular universalism. Marx, Engels, Lenin, Mao—all as central to the black elite's extended curriculum as the liberal humanist's Shakespeare—provided him with an indispensable theory of how revolutionary change might arise out of the colonial system's antagonistic contradictions, and about the vanguard role of the national bourgeoisie in such a struggle.

Yet the local Communist Party's belief in the triumph of the human spirit over oppression, its conviction that a people's democracy where "all persons live together in harmony" was achievable in South Africa, extended and did not negate the values that Mandela learned from Dr. Kerr, Victorian poetry, and Shakespeare. As with the influence on him of Gandhi's thought, the diverse social structures and political traditions to which he was exposed created in him not merely a layering of values that might be inflected as the situation demanded. Another effect of this heterogeneity of political formation was that certain priorities and ideals intertwined and were reinforced, most particularly in Mandela's case the vision of a secular, classless, *and* racism-free society that sustained him from the 1940s.

· · · · ·

"[T]he freedom movement in South Africa believes that hard and swift blows should be delivered with the full weight of the masses of the people, who alone furnish us with one absolute guarantee that the freedom flames now burning in the country shall never be extinguished."

*Nelson Mandela, from "A Land Ruled by the Gun" (1962)*

· · · · ·

## Diasporic Affiliation or African Patrimony

Mandela's commitment to extending black self-representation through mass political mobilization, beginning at a time that coincided more or less with the early civil rights movement in the United States, inevitably raises the question of his affiliation to African-American and Pan-African traditions of political thought. Is it possible to place Mandela in relation to a network of diasporic African intellectuals preoccupied with ideas of black self-making, of Africans as citizens of the modern world? His Fort Hare mentor Z. K. Matthews who had studied in the United States, acknowledged a debt to Booker T. Washington's reformist ideas of black self-improvement. And, a more tenuous link, Mandela valued W. E. Henley's inspirational "Invictus" (Latin for undefeated), that was beloved, too, of Marcus Garvey, the Jamaican champion of "Back to Africa" ideas. Garvey, like Mandela, probably first encountered the 1875 poem in a colonial school-reader and cherished it as a watchword for self-empowerment.

African-American thought on racial discrimination strongly influenced the group of educationalists, lawyers, and journalists who in 1912 founded the ANC. Self-made as intellectuals, yet brought up to respect literary and political traditions imported from elsewhere, they found special corroboration and encouragement in African-American writing: Booker T.'s belief that education advanced black social progress; W. E. B. DuBois's speculations on the twentieth-century problem of "the color line."

Alongside the African-Americans and Shakespeare, from the 1920s South African black intellectuals and professionals also included on their reading list Pan-African nationalist theories fomenting closer to home, most notably in West Africa. This range of influence is clearly discernible in the speeches of the ANCYL theoretician Anton Lembede who, decades before Biko, invoked an organic, continental black identity and urged Africans to develop self-reliance by citing Garvey, DuBois, and Xhosa heroes of the past, as well as Shakespeare. The cosmopolitan world of Sophiatown that regarded all Africa as the audience for its music and journalism, undoubtedly bore the mark of all these influences, of English literature, American jazz, and ideas of Pan-African unity.

Yet, even though Mandela familiarized himself with the writing on liberation of nationalist leaders like Kwame Nkrumah of the Gold Coast (later Ghana), and the widely influential Pan-Africanist George Padmore, he, unlike some of his political friends and forebears, does not fit into the transnational African lineage in obvious ways. He remained till relatively late a Xhosa patriot as well as an African nationalist with a specifically South African focus. His 1962 and 1964 court speeches make clear that he saw himself as indebted first and foremost to indigenous, not imported, traditions of resistance struggle, even where African models were being transmitted back to Africa via the diaspora. He spoke of the "wars fought by our ancestors in defense of the fatherland" as inspiring him with the hope "to serve my people and make my own humble contribution to their freedom struggle."

Such exclusive loyalties were no doubt shaped in part by the special restrictions of internal colonialism under which a rurally educated black nationalist like Mandela operated, which meant his access to the major channels of Pan-Africanist thinking, though not blocked, was not always direct, certainly not in the 1940s. So it was the urbanite Sisulu rather than Mandela who made a point in this early period of following wider African nationalist developments in the papers (and who first read up on India's long freedom struggle). This relative distance from a specifically pan-nationalist affiliation helps explain how, unlike other early Africanists in the ANC, Mandela became increasingly more, rather than less, open to a heterogeneous array of political influences, in addition to nationalism: to socialist and communist thought, and to theories of resistance drawn from India.

This for Mandela was one of the drawbacks of later Black Consciousness thinking, that it was too closely influenced by African-American and European existential ideas of black self-determination when there were heroes of resistance to admire who had struggled closer to home: the Khoikhoi leader Willem Uithaalder, Moshoeshoe, Cetshwayo. The clenched fist salute, too, he was anxious to point out, far from first being raised as a Black Power sign, was used by the ANC in 1960. (Relatedly, his interest in the Afrikaans language lay in its indigeneity, in the fact that it was a language that had grown on South African soil, with black roots.) On his 1990 triumphal tour of America, Mandela was anxious to mark his distance even from Martin Luther King's ideal of nonviolence as having been untenable for South Africa in the 1960s. By contrast, he was always ready to acknowledge his debts to that other champion of nonviolence, Gandhi, from whose political strategies King in the 1950s, too, borrowed. King's struggle in this respect ran in parallel with Mandela's.

In his 1976 BCM essay, Mandela comfortably praises Gandhi's "quest for unity" as one emulated by the ANC, and in his biography describes the prison hunger strike as a tactic adapted from Gandhi.

Social cooperation, consensual government, community unity, cultural dignity—Mandela's core values as a nationalist, he repeatedly claimed, were embedded in local and regional African traditions and practices, and enshrined in the homilies of oral narrative. Indeed, his very assertion of the importance of what is indigenous and local is itself profoundly nationalist. It is also at the same time typically modern and synthetic, in that the value of the local and patrimonial only fully emerges to one separated from their customary background whether by an education in Western individualism, or by the relatively alienated life of the city. This recognition does not, however, take away from the consistency with which Mandela always upheld in particular the traditional ideal—but equally the reinvented tradition—of *ubuntu*, of mutual responsibility and human fellowship.

· · · · ·

"Passive resistance is a method of securing rights by personal suffering; it is the reverse of resistance by arms. When I refuse to do a thing that is repugnant to my conscience, I use soul-force [*satyagraha*]. For instance, the government of the day has passed a law which is applicable to me. I do not like it. If, by using violence, I force the government to repeal the law, I am employing what may be termed body-force. If I do not obey the law, and accept the penalty for its breach, I use soul-force. It involves sacrifice of self."

*M. K. Gandhi, from "Passive Resistance,"* Hind Swaraj *(1910)*

· · · · ·

## Warriors for Freedom: Gandhi, Nehru, Mandela

In histories of twentieth-century freedom struggles the names Gandhi and Mandela often appear paired, as two sides of the same anticolonial, nationalist coin (more so than either does with King). Both leaders, in the standard interpretation, achieved independence for their countries through largely nonviolent means, though Gandhi's commitment to passive resistance is recognized to have been uncompromising in a way that Mandela could not—and did not seek to—match. Moreover, reinforcing this link, Mandela is perceived not only to have shared in Gandhi's vision of a common humanity transcending racial, cultural, and other differences, but in fact to have derived strategies of nonconstitutional protest directly from the Indian leader's legacy, forged of course on South African soil. In words of homage dedicated to Mandela since his retirement, whether by political opponents like Tony Leon or supporters like Nadine Gordimer, the comparison with Gandhi, and the references to a shared secular saintliness, are now almost *de rigueur*. It was in recognition of this widely acknowledged debt that Mandela in 2000 was co-awarded India's Gandhi Peace Prize.

The fellow feeling that flows from Mandela toward his anticolonial counterpart M. K. Gandhi is undeniable, though hindsight does accentuate its extent. As far back as the early 1950s in the vibrantly interconnected world of cosmopolitan Sophiatown, Mandela was well known to be not only a stylish dresser, as will be seen, but also "an unwavering adherent of Mahatma Gandhi's nonviolent philosophy." Like Gandhi, Mandela from the beginning of his career as a politicized lawyer stood for, and stood up for, human dignity, thereby exposing the hypocrisy of the opposition, who tended to claim the moral high ground in this respect. Like Gandhi, too, Mandela deployed nonviolent strategies in order to achieve his political aims, though Gandhi did so more persistently, under less repressive duress. Mandela had a portrait of Gandhi hanging alongside pictures of the Allied leaders Stalin, Roosevelt, and Churchill, and of the storming of the Winter Palace, in his first Orlando home. From 1964 he emphasized that a Gandhist philosophy of toleration had shaped the ANC's liberationist "school of thought." A remarkable historical parallel solders the link between them: both spent periods of imprisonment in Johannesburg's infamous Fort prison (now the site of the Constitutional Court)—Gandhi in 1908 when campaigning for Indian rights; Mandela in 1956 and 1962.

However, looked at more closely, the apparent similarity between the two leaders, though it rests on a broad *commitment to nonconstitutional action* in the name of a higher justice, is complicated by a number of factors. Not least among these is, first, that Gandhi (1869–1948) is chronologically and in terms of influence Mandela's political precursor. Second, Mandela is only one among Gandhi's African heirs, and a belated one at that. Kenneth Kaunda and Kwame Nkrumah, too, influentially invoked his passive resistance legacy. Third, and most important, there is the fact that Mandela's relationship of influence with Gandhi from the start entailed a situation of difficult affiliation rather than direct tribute. To Mandela the relationship was always complicated by the conflicting claims of first Africanist and then socialist allegiance and, finally, by the commitment to "armed propaganda": "there came a point in our struggle when the [oppressor's] brute force . . . could no longer be countered through passive resistance alone." Therefore, when post-1990 Mandela commented in a comparative way on Gandhi's importance and made reference to the "sacred" qualities of this freedom warrior, he also described him as a citizen of *both* South Africa *and* India, hence as claiming a different, dual set of cultural and nationalist ties.

If anything, there are in terms of character and approach stronger links of affiliation between Mandela and Jawaharlal Nehru, India's first Prime Minister, a Gandhi follower, and a partial contemporary, as a reading of the latter's *The Discovery of India* (1946) and, especially, his 1936 *Autobiography* alongside Mandela's life-writing confirms. When in search of inspirational histories of liberation struggle in the 1940s, Mandela turned to Nehru as well as Gandhi, finding in him a political pragmatism and strong personal discipline that corresponded with his own, as well as a congenial emotive connection to his nation India. By 1947, the year of Indian independence, Nehru had become for Mandela a glittering epitome of an inspirational leader.

Mandela shared with Nehru, too, an admiration for the rationality of socialism, and state modernization, and may also have identified with his conviction of messianic purpose as a leader, as expressed in his autobiography, accompanied by a strong sense of personal isolation, "an exile's feeling." Moreover, Nehru's acceptance of the principle of justified retaliation, and the frustration he experienced with respect to Gandhi's determined pacifism, resonated with Mandela's always-tactical, qualified adoption of a passive resistance stance. On Robben Island, he kept Nehru's—and Gandhi's—prison memoirs in mind as examples of how to maintain mental resilience through the discipline of reading and writing. He was no doubt self-consciously building on these points of commonality with Nehru when he borrowed from his prose in his own early speeches and articles. From the epilogues of Nehru's *Discovery* and *Autobiography*, and his collection of essays, *The Unity of India* (1942), he derived some of the governing phrases and images of his career: *No Easy Walk to Freedom*, *The Struggle Is My Life*.

Yet Mandela's affiliation to Nehru is as complicated by his Africanist loyalties as is his tie to Gandhi, definitely so at the time of initial influence, but also thereafter. The divergences between the Indian leaders and Mandela go deeper than differences in historical context and national temperament alone suggest. Even those who claim a continuous line of inheritance from Gandhi to Mandela, concede that during his early period of ANCYL activism, his nationalism took predominantly exclusive, Africanist forms. It was noticeable that, within the ANCYL,

**Like Mandela, Jawaharlal Nehru** (1889–1964), the first prime minister of India, was an enthusiastic supporter of the social reforms promulgated by Gandhi—whose own first exposure to racial injustice took place in South Africa. This photograph shows Gandhi and Nehru together at the All-India Congress in Bombay in 1946.

Mandela always lagged behind his colleague Sisulu in forging common cause with the South African Indian Congress (SAIC), and local Indian leaders like Yusuf Dadoo. For him, the ANC alone was the embodiment of the African will against oppression. Up till the late 1940s he was openly suspicious of collaborating with both "Indians" and whites, on the grounds that their representatives' expertise gave them an advantage over African leaders "out of all proportion to their numbers." It was a class- as well as a race-based point. Although the ANC had always taken the line that opposition to white racialism must entail a refusal to assert black racialism, Mandela was exercised to promote more marginalized black African political claims first and foremost. For him, too, many South African Indians had found in communism a viable anticolonial political critique, whereas he as a fervent nationalist was at this stage unconvinced by communism. As far on as 1950 he and other African nationalists were involved in breaking up meetings of ANC and SAIC communists— "tearing up posters and capturing the microphone"—on the grounds that communism was un-African. African workers, they felt, were oppressed on the grounds of race, not class.

To understand properly the comparative axis that putatively connects the two leaders, Mandela and Gandhi, it is important to ask what it was, in the space of a few years, that noticeably changed Mandela's way of thinking. How was it that he became a proponent, if for a limited period, of Gandhist passive resistance? Post-1918, it must first be recognized, nationalist movements throughout Africa saw the Indian leader's noncooperation as *the* effective mode of anti-imperialism above all others. In a context of growing international support for colonial self-determination and of the fight against Nazism, Gandhi's Congress movement was widely perceived as having brought the British Empire to its knees through nonviolence. In a key 1949 pamphlet Kwame Nkrumah defined what he called Positive Action, directed at self-government, as "the adoption of all legitimate and constitutional means . . . [to] attack the forces of imperialism . . . as used by Gandhi in India." Guided by Nkrumah and the Caribbean activist George Padmore, and recognizing the challenges posed by militant resistance, African leaders at the Fifth Pan-African Congress held in Manchester in 1945 *all* expressed a strong adherence to Gandhist nonviolence.

In the relatively closed South African context, another crucial fact underpinning Mandela's change of heart, is that the ANC had, almost from its inception, experienced forms of interaction with Gandhist policies, a cooperation explained by his having worked in South Africa as a lawyer-activist for nearly twenty-one years, 1893–1914. In Mandela's retrospective words, "The Indian struggle, in a sense, is rooted in the African"— and this despite the discomfort expressed by Gandhi and his followers at being classed with "Natives" while in prison. As *Hind Swaraj* (1910) and *Satyagraha in South Africa* (1928) clarify, Gandhi developed in the country his doctrine of implacable passive resistance to imperial oppression, based on a thoroughgoing spiritual critique of Western civilization: its materialist ideologies of progress, its "predominance of might over right." Practically, Gandhi first in Natal and later in the Transvaal (the provinces where indentured laborers had been concentrated) organized Indians to protest against restrictions on their rights to land, business practice, and citizenship through symbolic acts of refusal (certificate burning, marches), along with morally committed law-breaking. *Satyagraha*, or "soul-force," the nonviolent resistance to injustice, Mandela observed in 2000, meant that Gandhi's was a "complete" critique not only of colonial relations of power, but also of the industrial capital that fueled colonialism, its structures of economic exploitation, its ethic of self-interest.

As the journalism of its founders demonstrates, the ANC had always been keenly aware of the influential nonviolent operations of its Indian nationalist counterparts. It is interesting, however, that a Gandhist mode within ANC activism was most strongly expressed in its Women's League activities: in their reliance on petitions, marches, chanting, public derision, and mass silences; that is, on *symbolic action*, culminating in their 1956 March on Pretoria. In the 1950s, Mandela's engagement with passive resistance strategies was consistently reinforced and amplified by ANC Women's League and the Federation of South African Women protests. As early as 1913, African women in the Orange Free State had, apparently spontaneously, expressed their rejection of the extension of pass laws to women by dumping pass books at police stations and giving themselves up for arrest.

In respect of the specific Mandela-Gandhi comparison, this situation of parallel activism involving Africans and Indians is of central importance. In the mid-1940s, as Mandela, Sisulu, and others were developing Congress into a broad-based national liberation movement, the Indian Congresses in Natal and the Transvaal, too, were powerfully organizing against repressive laws applied to Indians. Two of Mandela's fellow law students, Ismail Meer and J. N. Singh, spearheaded the 1946 passive resistance campaign against Smuts's "ghetto laws" restricting Indians to particular urban areas, so reawakening Gandhist strategies from earlier in the century. Mandela, who sometimes stayed at Kathrada's inner-city lodgings, Kholvad house, participated there in lively discussions with a variety of campaigners, Gandhists as well as radical Christians and communists. Yet, concerned as he was for African freedom, he at this point (unlike Sisulu) *still* took a strictly observer role vis-à-vis the Indians' politics. To him, until *satyagraha* could be projected onto a multiracial platform, it remained identified as a means of agitation for an ethnic minority alone.

What changed was, in a nutshell, the victory of the Afrikaner National Party in 1948, with its explicit policy of codifying white domination and racial segregation as law. Now a proportional relationship developed in the country between the expression of nonwhite protest and the level of white repression. As resistance grew in intensity, so did the state's expression of its "formidable apparatus of force and coercion," in Mandela's words. Indian and African leaders, including Sisulu, had in 1949 been forced to stand together to express communal grief following riots in Durban in which Africans turned on Indians, perceiving them, within the punishing hierarchy of apartheid, to be their exploiters. Mandela held himself apart from this joint action, yet the broad front then demonstrated had the same effect on him as his new collaboration with outlawed SACP members, dramatizing that there was benefit to be gained from expressing solidarity in practice. The unforgiving mobilization of the apartheid laws had forced opponents of the regime into recognizing the strengths that lay in mutual cooperation.

In 1949 the ANCYL launched a Program of Action that involved the deployment of unmistakably Gandhist "weapons"—boycott, civil disobedience, peaceful marches, noncooperation (strategies Gandhi had himself cooperatively "borrowed" from Irish nationalists and British suffragettes). These weapons, it was believed, would not immediately become the targets of violent state repression as would more conventional methods, yet could not be ignored in the way that ANC petitioning had been dismissed in the past. In 1950 the ANC directly cooperated with the SAIC and SACP in organizing a May Day strike (which Mandela did not back), and then a National Day of Protest against the Suppression of Communism Act (which he did). Always concerned that the ANC spearhead any initiative, the June Day of Protest was the first occasion on which he worked alongside Indian comrades and future friends like Ahmed Kathrada, so laying the ground for a new coalition politics. He perceived that the "Gandhian model" did not necessarily demand a full moral commitment but was for an unarmed people principally a tactic "to be used as the situation demanded," most dynamically so in mid-1952.

The massively successful, four-month ANC-SAIC Defiance Campaign was first formally motivated by Sisulu at the thirty-fifth annual ANC conference in December 1951, where M.K. Gandhi's son Manilal was present, in order "to force the government to repeal six unjust laws." Symbolically timed to coincide with the tercentennial celebrations of white settlement, the first protest procession marched on June 26, 1952, led by veteran Gandhist Nana Sita, its objective peacefully to violate the state's area restrictions and petty apartheid laws. Protesters walked singing into racially segregated residential areas without the requisite permits, and so into jail. In *Drum*'s description: "Everywhere they marched quietly and did what they were told by the police, singing hymns with their thumbs up. They always informed the police beforehand to make sure they would be arrested."

As the Campaign's national volunteer-in-chief, Mandela, with Maulvi Cachalia as his deputy, traveled the country, mainly on trains, recruiting both new and more established constituencies of supporters. For the first time he learned about his own capacity for mass outreach, for persuading protesters to remain consistent in their nonviolence (which was fundamental to the Campaign's success). He came to realize, as had Gandhi on his many railway journeys across India, that the reach of inspirational leadership can be measured through the number and power of the symbolic goals it sets.

The collaborative Defiance Campaign remains a major success in the ANC's historical annals. Over 8,500 defiers of all races came forward, with a total of 2,354 arrests. Congress was turned into a mass movement based in passive resistance with a burgeoning membership. Cross-nationalist and inter-movement cooperation, and the symbolic eloquence of nonviolent protest—singing, marching, dancing—was never more persuasively demonstrated in South Africa than at this point. The mass mobilization had allowed the ANC to maintain a moral advantage, yet also instilled in its members a sense of agency and comradeship. As for Mandela, due to a series of banning orders in the decade following, he was never again, until his release from prison forty years later, so publicly to be associated with a particular activist line. An important indication of how central the advocacy of peaceful protest became to ANC politics and rhetoric is that in 1969, long after Sharpeville, the ANC journal *Sechaba* felt obliged to cite an obscure 1938 Declaration on the defense of rights by Gandhi to justify the turn to armed struggle. "Violence," he had there noted, was preferable to "the emasculation of a whole race."

The narrative of political influence connecting Mandela to Gandhi outlined above can be concentrated down to the following areas of borrowing and linked activity. First, as regards their role and style as leaders, both Gandhi and Mandela, though at different historical moments, powerfully channeled in their respective countries the great wave of anti-imperial activity that from the First World War began to change the geopolitical map. They did so, first and foremost, by working to create *popular mass movements* in which they eclectically deployed, at one and the same time, not only the peaceable aspects of indigenous cultures (weaving, tactics of communal discussion), but also, equally, modern media technologies and the power of the image. Both were shrewd exploiters of their own myth, to the extent that even the inner, private spaces of their lives were turned outward to the public in service of the myth. Like Gandhi, Mandela delighted in using the language of dress (less so the language of the body) to symbolize his politics, as will be seen. In this, however, he did not so much learn from Gandhi *per se*, as that he developed, through his prison years, his youthful delight in sartorial display into an almost intuitive, postmodern-seeming sensitivity to the media image. Fatima Meer once flippantly commented: "Gandhi took off his clothes. Nelson *loves* his clothes."

Then, though both Gandhi and Mandela worked *against* the Victorian (and then Edwardian) empire and its aftermath, both men, too, were in certain ways its products. They were schooled as black Englishmen within empire's educational institutions and trained as lawyers within its legal systems. In consequence, both were shaped by the complicated conjunctions of social pathways and political pilgrimages that empire generated, and felt the impact of, as Edward Said has said, the dynamic cultural activity such conjunctions unleashed. Despite Gandhi's outright rejection of modern civilization, he shared with Mandela a *respect for British traditions* of justice and democracy, and an appreciation of aspects of European culture, especially of the great books of the liberal West. Gandhi emotively cited Tennyson to persuade the British to Quit India; Mandela recited Henley by way of self-motivation in prison. Both espoused the quintessentially Victorian virtues of self-help and self-reliance.

Furthermore, as part of their *humanizing vision*, both had the ability (Mandela the more so after his release) eclectically to synthesize countercultural and counter-hegemonic strategies with dominant concepts and views, as the situation demanded. As a striking illustration, Gandhi and Mandela, who both found themselves pitted against the forces of Boer nationalism, in 1899–1900 and 1948–90 respectively, discerned in the Boer's determined, often symbolic resistance to empire important lessons for their own political struggles. From the time that he took up armed resistance, Mandela, for example, would quote as an authority *Commando* (1929), the war memoir of the Boer guerrilla Denys Reitz.

Finally, among the most striking areas of commonality is the willingness in the cases of both Gandhi and Mandela to forge links of solidarity with other nationalist groups, that is, to translate their political relations from a hierarchical onto a lateral or *fraternal axis*. While Gandhi adopted the Irish nationalists' use of boycott, Mandela and Sisulu, in borrowing from the SAIC's tactics of noncooperation, palpably discovered the boost to morale and strategy that emerged from anticolonialist hand-holding. As Mandela later acknowledged from prison, it was important that exclusive forms of nationalism give way to the recognition of the *brotherhood of nations*. He and his fellow activists were in this respect in the advantageous position of encountering Gandhist activism as an on-site resource, a living, working practice in South Africa. In an instance of perhaps the closest "cheek-by-jowl" collaboration that anticolonial history has yet seen, they developed passive resistance in association with activists who themselves had worked with Gandhi, and so moved at once tactically and symbolically against the state's segregationist logic.

The main divergence between Mandela's and Gandhist politics of course rises out of their contrasting views on armed struggle. Whereas Gandhi rejected violence out of hand, Mandela grew keenly aware as the

1950s wore on that Gandhist passive resistance had become untenable in an increasingly more authoritarian South Africa. A new ideological and strategic departure was called for, especially after Sharpeville. In so far as an African's life outside the tribal homelands had been rendered unlawful by definition, the recourse to violence increasingly appeared as a legitimate right.

Yet ultimately the link between Gandhi and Mandela lies not so much in the obvious area of passive resistance as in their opportunistic, tactical, and always media-savvy response to circumstance, informed by an eclectic range of political and philosophical influences. Neither was at any point consistent in their responses, unless it was in their emphasis on *self-restraint*, this supremely Victorian quality of self-mastery and operation within the rule of law which they derived from the British colonial education they shared.

· · · · ·

"What is the real nature of this violence? We have seen that it is the intuition of the colonized masses that their liberation must, and can only, be achieved by force."

*Frantz Fanon, from "Concerning Violence,"*
The Wretched of the Earth *(1961)*

· · · · ·

## The Move to Armed Struggle

Nelson Mandela and the ANC made their commitment to armed struggle in the early 1960s because it appeared that other modes of resistance, to which they in principle remained committed, had closed down. Peaceful protest had proved powerless against an authority quick to the trigger and impervious to public opinion. In June 1961 Mandela captured this restriction of resistance options with a traditional proverb: "The attacks of the wild beast cannot be averted with only bare hands."

To guide his organization in making its difficult decision Mandela read widely in the literature on war and revolution available to him, including Mao Tse-tung, Louis Taruc, and Clausewitz. Yet in the various biographical accounts of this time there is one glaring omission from the reading list: the name of the Paris-trained Martiniquan Frantz Fanon, easily the most important post-1950 theorist of anticolonial violence, who had already drawn wide attention in francophone Africa.

For the ANC, the Algerian freedom struggle against the local white settler regime had for some time been perceived to exhibit strong parallels with South Africa's. On Mandela's African travels he came into contact with Front de Libération Nationale officials who had fought for the independence of Algeria, recently won, for whose left-wing Fanon had served as an angry spokesperson. At Oujda in Morocco, an Algerian military base close to the border, he heard Ahmed Ben Bella the guerrilla leader, soon to be first President of an independent Algeria, rally his troops and call for the fight against imperialism to be extended across Africa. In this context, though Mandela never mentions Fanon by name, it is difficult to believe that he did not feel in some capacity the transformative force of his ideas.

The shift from passive to active resistance in Mandela is often described in terms suggesting a move from a Gandhist position to a greater proximity to Fanon. Fanon's approach to the overthrow of imperial power, based on his time working as a psychiatrist in revolutionary

Algeria, was bracingly combative: the colonized, he believed, should resist the colonizer to the death, with violence; their entire sensibility should be focused on this rejection. For Gandhi, by contrast, repelling the colonizer with force was to stoop to his techniques of oppression. These two opposed traditions of resistance theory, advocating nonco-operation and armed overthrow, bifurcate postcolonial thinking to this day. The question for this book is whether Mandela saw the distinction between the traditions as clear-cut, and, specifically, whether his radicalization was supported by actual influence from Fanon. There is no doubt that, some ten years on from the ANC's move to arms, Steve Biko's BCM, with its outright rejection of white values, demonstrated a clear debt to Fanon's fiercely nationalist and anticolonial manifesto *The Wretched of the Earth* (1961).

When in early 1962 Mandela canvassed prevailing ideas on military resistance across Africa, he was *already* convinced that the only remaining recourse for South Africa's marginalized majority was violent retaliation. The path toward this decision had been difficult, necessitating delicate negotiations with Gandhist and Christian ANC leaders, but after Sharpeville and the May 1961 suppression of the national strike, Mandela saw no alternative. The ANC's arsenal of noncooperative responses had been exhausted. Moreover, in the wake of the formation of the PAC, it was important to offer leadership to the ANC's more militant groupings. As he along with others wrote in MK's admirably restrained December 16, 1961, manifesto: "The time comes in the life of any nation when there remain only two choices: submit or fight. That time has now come in South Africa." Nonviolent resistance would still be propagated by the ANC, yet it would now be complimented with a graduated program of armed resistance, led by a group separate from, though affiliated to, the parent body. Small cadres of saboteurs would be able to move against the state with greater dexterity than a peacefully marching crowd.

In his first international speech, "A Land Ruled by the Gun," given at the January 1962 PAFMECA (later OAU) conference in Addis Ababa, Mandela sought to justify the ANC's controversial turn to violence, its "sharpening" of its "less effective" political weapons (while reassuring African supporters that civil disobedience would continue). Like Fanon in *his* polemical address in support of anticolonial violence given to the 1958 All-Africa People's Conference, Mandela, an admirer of *Julius Caesar*, gives a careful exposition of the stages of increasing violence the African majority has suffered. As part of this exposition he suggests, as famously does Fanon, that the colonized system's pervasive "atmosphere of violence" is the creation of the colonizer alone, and that in this situation the colonized has no choice but to reject the system absolutely. Any compromise or attempt to come to terms will simply reinforce oppression: "only violence pays." Mandela's summary of South Africa's anti-imperialist struggle builds gradually toward a short, uncompromising paragraph encapsulating the injunction that "hard and swift blows" need *now* to be delivered. Strategically framed as a response to a Mark Antony–like rhetorical question concerning what role freedom movements should take against the state's "multiple onslaughts"—"Can anyone, therefore, doubt the role that the freedom movements should play in view of this hideous conspiracy?"—Mandela's charged language is at this point distinctly reminiscent of Fanon. Fanon's own 1958 conference speech, given as a riposte to Kwame Nkrumah's influential advocacy of Positive Action stopping short of violence, had been unequivocal in making its central point: the native's violence was not merely necessary but self-transforming.

(The speech, which cited Sharpeville as a reminder of colonialism's over-kill, was developed into the chapter "Concerning Violence" that forms the core of *The Wretched of the Earth*.)

Published in French, a language Mandela could not read, *The Wretched of the Earth* did not appear in English translation till 1965, by which time he was already in prison. Yet, as these parallels suggest, it seems likely that he would on more than one occasion on his African tour, most probably in Addis Ababa as well as Morocco, have been exposed to Fanon's ideas, even if at several removes. He explicitly refers both to the 1958 Conference and to Nkrumah's defensive 1960 Positive Action conference in "A Land Ruled by the Gun": he would have known about the debates that had taken place at both venues. In this context it seems fitting that MK with Mandela at its head was established in 1961, the year of *The Wretched of the Earth*.

Though Mandela would not cease privately to believe that active resistance had in practice to be calibrated against passive, at this point in the early 1960s he would have agreed with Fanon, had they met, that colonial brutality had exhausted the options available to nonviolence. Sharpeville crops up in his conference talk, too, as a graphic example of such brutality. Retaliatory violence had become for Mandela the primary (for Fanon the only) means of obliterating the Manichean, us-versus-them politics of the repressive state. The binary choice was to "submit or fight," yet to submit effectively meant canceling one's nationalist impulses, which was unthinkable. The alternative was to resort to a self-defining, disciplined counter-violence.

Taking a chronological view of his career across five decades, 1950 to 2000, we see Mandela tracing an ideological parabola away from his early Gandhist phase, toward a support for armed resistance, and then, at the last, turning back to nonviolent ideas of political negotiation and compromise. As this might suggest, within a postcolonial framework he represents an interesting point of encounter between two, apparently opposed approaches to resistance: Fanon's advocacy of cathartic violence and Gandhi's promotion of noncooperation, the weapons of the weak. In so far as he lived through two political lifetimes, the optimistic era of postcolonial independence and the more pessimistic, post–Cold War period of capitulation to global capitalism, Mandela essentially experienced the differential impact of these two approaches at first hand and at times played them off against one another. Now he spoke of African self-expression by means of the destruction of the colonizer's world; now he supported national self-realization through the embrace and incorporation of that world.

From the point of view of 1961, Mandela's willingness to espouse armed struggle appears, by definition, to be a clean break with his mid-career pacifism. Yet there is another way of casting his change of heart. If anything, Mandela's anticolonial and antiracist positions across his long career represent sliding points on his ideological scale. To appreciate this fully, it is worth bearing in mind that active and passive modes of resistance generally work interdependently as strategies and therefore are best assessed comparatively, in relation to one another. As an illustration, Gandhi viewed *satyagraha* as active, far from passive: to him it was performative, energized, relentless; passive only in the sense of not involving arms.

As for Mandela, he and the other more radical ANC members were always intensely pragmatic about the uses of militancy. In many ways they had to be—MK was a notoriously ineffective guerrilla force. They were keenly aware, more so than Gandhi perhaps allowed, that nonviolence historically operated in dialectical tandem with outbreaks of violence, or what they called armed propaganda—the presentation, at least, of a front of armed resistance. Rather than being a conclusive shift away from passive resistance, Mandela's move to armed struggle entailed a tacit recognition that noncooperation could not thrive as a politics without the accompaniment of some form of militancy.

Throughout, there was a determined logic to Mandela's position. In his Treason Trial defense he made clear that the ANC's defiance campaigns were intended to persuade the government to agree, "Let's talk." Thirty years on, he continued to see armed resistance as a means of moving to the negotiation table while, at the same time, his shift toward *a dialogic ethic* never involved a complete renunciation of political violence. Indeed, it can be argued that a key reason why South Africa did not in the 1980s become the "bloodbath" that Mandela feared it might, was because the ANC was tireless in playing the threat of violence against nonviolence in mounting its opposition to the apartheid government. Its struggle was "multi-targeted," as Mandela explained in London as far back as 1962.

Yet to trace Gandhist or Fanonist, African-American or Nkrumah- esque influences on Mandela's political philosophy should not imply that his thought was merely belated. Influence translated from other cultural and political contexts can often produce intensive cross-border interaction, rather than what is called a derivative discourse. As in his sartorial displays, or his espousal of African-style negotiation, there was much in Mandela that looked like the mark of something from elsewhere (be it *ahimsa*/nonviolence or multiculturalism), but was always charismatically combined with more local practices. What was particularly innovative about his, say, Gandhist or Nehruvian approach, was that he was able to adapt it to suit South African conditions at the time. Moreover, there was much in that which influenced him which he did not find congenial and did not take on board, such as the strong antiwhite feeling that characterized 1960s African nationalism, or, as will be seen, Gandhi's feminization of resistance politics.

# FIVE

## Sophiatown Sophisticate

•

IN SOWETO POET OSWALD MTSHALI'S "The Detribalized," the fast-living *tsotsi* or gangster, the subject of the poem, who "hails from Sophiatown / Or Alexandra," is said to "know" imprisoned Mandela and Sobukwe but to care less. The poem is included in *Halala Madiba* (2006), an anthology of poems generally in praise of Mandela, apart from this one. Yet the apparent incongruity is appropriate. It emphasizes a central though sometimes neglected part of Mandela's sociopolitical formation, his coming-to-maturity in the exhilarating spaces of South Africa's largest city Johannesburg, lodestar of go-getting Africans: the townships of Alexandra and Orlando where he lived, and Fordsburg and Sophiatown where he socialized.

The culturally mixed environment of 1950s Kofifi or Sophiatown, its "swarming, cacophonous, strutting" inner-city streets, and the

**This 1958 photograph** gives an impression of the sartorial savvy Mandela began to display in the 1950s.

intellectual flowering that took place there, was arguably *as important* to Mandela's makeup as Gandhi's *satyagraha*, or the militant nationalism of post-war Africa. It certainly was here, in an environment self-consciously modeled on 1920s "Renaissance" Harlem, where penny whistle jazz and Africanized movie slang rang out all night long from the shebeens, that Mandela was exposed to the social flexibility and creative collisions—the *discrepant attachments*—that late colonial modernity in Africa involved. It was here that he became the master of what we now term postmodern display.

· · · · ·

"The undying spirit of the mining town, born of large freedoms and given to flamboyant forms of expression."

*Herman Charles Bosman, from "Johannesburg Riots" (1945)*

· · · · ·

## City Streets

At the cosmopolitan crossing-point between transatlantic influences and liberal mission-school values that was mid-century black Johannesburg, Mandela acquired the eloquence, street savvy, and smart suits—in short, the public demeanor—that allowed him, a rural youth, to remake himself as an "African gentleman," a citizen of the city. The cultural vibrancy in particular of Sophiatown communicated itself though the whole of Johannesburg, including densely packed Orlando, at the heart of today's Soweto. Here, in crowded streets of small brick houses, Mandela adopted the "Edwardian" style for which in the 1990s he became famous—the pressed clothes, correct manners, and modulated public speech—and fused these with the self-control of his school upbringing. In these streets he developed the vision of positive success—that Africans belonged to the modern state and the future—that sustained him across his prison years.

Here, too, he was exposed not only to compelling images of African-American self-assertion from film and jazz, but also to the edgy defensiveness of African nationalist machismo more generally. The aristocratic country boy discovered the intoxicating charge of projecting a modern urban image that was based on professional shine and outward show yet relatively little wealth. Here, finally, in the crucible that was freehold Alexandra-Orlando-Sophiatown before the segregationist laws of the 1950s fully took hold, before apartheid became shrewd and brutal, the *noncombative multiracialism* or *interculturalism* of the ANC was alchemized. Although this context is relatively neglected by biographers keen to emphasize his patrician background and Methodist upbringing as key factors shaping Mandela's outlook, the "match" between the cultural vibrancy of rapidly urbanizing Africa and the debonair young lawyer tempts further exploration. It is definitely indicative that in the early 1950s Mandela above other prominent Africans became the figure promoted by *Drum* magazine and its white editorship as the embodiment of Congress politics.

Even more than the African residential areas of Alexandra or Orlando, or the Indian-and-Colored suburb of Fordsburg, the glamorous if seedy Sophiatown of the 1950s, epicenter of urban South Africa, was a uniquely innovative, interactive place, twanging with short-fuse optimism and creative energy, especially in music and journalism. Pastimes of choice were street-side gambling, live music, street shoot-outs, ballroom dancing—in which Mandela and many others participated—and, most glamorous and streetwise of all, boxing, his sport of choice. This unifying culture was made possible by Kofifi's "black spot" status: until the Group Areas Act and the forced removals of the mid-1950s, it was a township where black Africans could, unusually, own property and gain access to a variety of cultural channels, Asian and diasporic African alike. The slums that Alan Paton condemned in his classic *Cry, the Beloved Country* (1949) as a cesspit of prostitution and gang violence, the ruin of the "true" rural African, were located here, yet what he overlooked about the society was its remarkable openness and resourcefulness. Urban life, as Mandela himself acknowledged, abraded tribal differences.

At Sophiatown parties, white journalists famously mingled with black poets and Indian film critics. On its pavements philosophers rubbed shoulders with pickpockets and businessmen. In their music the Jazz Maniacs and the African Ink Spots, and solo artists like Isaac Nkosi and Dolly Radebe, paid tribute to African-American performers: Count Basie, Duke Ellington, Louis Armstrong. The small black middle class lived cheek-by-jowl not only with factory workers but, more unusually, a criminal underclass, called the African aristocracy, whose conspicuous consumption represented a bold defiance of township squalor. At this time of pass restrictions most urban Africans lived, perforce, on the wrong side of the law: denied basic facilities, many believed that achievement was measured in a glitzy look or style. In this environment Mandela as a lawyer in training, an incarnation of community aspirations, felt the social imperative of wearing elegant three-piece suits from Markhams. With his charisma and intense responsiveness to others, he grew keenly aware of the people's hunger for rallying symbols of their leaders.

Almost all reminiscences of the Sophiatown period testify to its cultural syncretism and extraordinary spirit. "Sophiatown [had] all the exuberant youth of Shakespeare's London," wrote *Drum* editor Anthony Sampson. "Over our dead bodies" was a slogan of the 1954–5 anti-eviction campaign. The zestful mingling that was Kofifi and its surroundings became fundamental to how Mandela (till 1948 an exclusivist nationalist) presented himself: that is, to the many-sided political personality he projected, *and* to his knowledge of what *being* a personality involved. In Sophiatown and Fordsburg he gained insight into both cultural *mixedness* and the *performance* of mixedness. He saw how, for the duration of a shebeen evening in Back of the Moon or 39 Steps, or at a jazz show by Dollar Brand or Dudu Pukwana at Uncle Joe's café, the divides of apartheid were briefly transcended, their leakiness exploited. Meetings across the color bar, whether casual or professional, private or political, were buoyed both by the daring represented by such encounters, and by a heady post-war idealism, a conviction that social harmony was possible, even in South Africa; indeed, that African leaders could remake the colonial state.

## The Making of a Modern Man

On arrival in Johannesburg, the youth who had been happy to press his well-dressed guardian's trousers and pleased at his gift of a striped, double-breasted suit, was struck by the glamour on show everywhere. Yet, as that image of the young Thembu aristocrat with the steam iron in his hand suggests, while this glamour may have appeared to him as the quintessential expression of the urban world, it was not entirely new. In the Transkei his guardian had used the material privileges that accrued to his position as chief to acquire the appurtenances of the modern African: not only the dress and car, but also the Western-style houses and university-educated advisors.

For the Christianized Chief Jongintaba, as for his relative Mandela, however, modernity was from the beginning to be defined not merely through material display, but through an ability to deploy different social registers and roles in relation to different audiences. For both men, "tradition" was never a simple inheritance from the past, but was understood as bound up with the modern present in complicated ways. The jagged, diverse effects of modernity importantly offered both powerful modes of resistance to the ways in which the apartheid system repressed Africans by retribalizing them, homogenizing them as "native" and "primitive."

Some biographical accounts of Mandela in the 1940s and 1950s suggest that he assumed an observer status relative to the teeming spectacle of the African city. Yet, looking more closely at where he socialized and how he dressed himself in these years, it becomes apparent that he not only delighted in the scene in an objective way, but also thrived in it, as an active if temperate participant. Indeed, some regarded him as insufficiently serious to be a politician. A teetotaler, he did not frequent the shebeens, yet he frequently ate in downtown restaurants like the Blue Lagoon and the Mauritian-owned Indian restaurant Kapitan's in Kort Street, where he developed a strong liking for prawn curry. From these vantage points he watched the passing display of well-heeled African fashion: *tsotsis* sporting Woodrow hats and Hagar slacks, cruising the streets in long, finned American cars.

A memorable image of Mandela at this time—"a tall, handsome man with hair parted in the middle . . . wearing a charcoal gray suit and [flashing] a big white-toothed smile of success" (etched in Lewis Nkosi's *Mandela's Ego*)—rightly evokes a man solicitous about his appearance, a follower of fashion. It is well known that throughout his career, even during prison visits, Mandela made a point of looking groomed. He especially enjoyed being the cynosure of women's eyes. When arrested in 1956, his strongest impression was of the relative physical unfitness of his fellow inmates. Few had "the symmetrical build of Shaka," he observed. This was undoubtedly a man not displeased with his own commanding physical stature (six feet three inches tall), aware that such height showed off a tailored suit to advantage. Fellow ANC campaigner Ellen Kuzwayo always remembered Nelson as the "glamorous one" among the troika he formed with Walter and Oliver.

· · · · ·

"I remember the glamorous Nelson Mandela of those years. The beautiful white silk scarf he wore around his neck stands out in my mind to this day. Walter Max Sisulu, on the other hand, was a hardy, down-to-earth man with practical clothing—typically a heavy coat and stout boots. Looking back, the third member of their trio, Oliver Tambo, acted as something of a balance, with his middle-of-the-road clothes!"

*Ellen Kuzwayo, from* Call Me Woman *(1985)*

· · · · ·

Mandela's Johannesburg years were, from the start, extremely busy, taken up first with study and legal work, and later, increasingly, with political activity, even during his banned periods. The waiting room at the Tambo and Mandela law offices was usually full to bursting. Yet, carrying out his duties as an attorney, he kept in mind the social and political importance for not only a black professional but also a politician of *looking the part*, of representing the modernity and confidence to which people aspired, of expressing urban possibility in all its multifacetedness. Although the ANC was relatively uninterested in debates about cultural politics, and the Sophiatown writers were, with equal but opposite force, dismissive of politicized art, ANC rallies in Sophiatown's Freedom Square juxtaposed style and politics, activism and art, in provocative, eye-catching ways that would certainly have impressed the image-conscious Nelson.

Tellingly, Mandela was known to be on first-name terms with many of the Johannesburg's gang leaders, such as Kortboy of the Americans. And how could he not, when ANC meetings were held in venues like the Moretsele Hotel, where the Americans went to have breakfast? He was conversant in the local patois, a "broken" mix of Afrikaans, Zulu, and Chicago-ese called *tsotsitaal* (English being deemed highfalutin). The many photographs of Mandela dating from this period, snapshots, studio pictures by Eli Weinberg and Peter Magubane, pay flamboyant testimony to the many roles he played and the different costumes he donned to play them. As well as the lawyer formally posed in his office with a vase of agapanthus, the photographs show the bridegroom, the Thembu chief, the public speaker, the activist, the boxer. Besides the range and cut of his suits, striking details include the differently patterned (including floral) ties he wore—decades before these became fashionable among young professionals.

But perhaps the most telling evidence of Mandela's intensive urban involvement was his passion for boxing, for which he trained for ninety minutes a day at an Orlando gym. Boxing was not merely the black majority's number one sport, drawing vast and varied audiences; it was also an activity demanding excellent physical form, individualism, strategy, and, above all, showmanship. It suited Mandela in every respect. Another reconstructed reminiscence of this time, Njabulo Ndebele's redemptive evocation *The Cry of Winnie Mandela*, reminds us that Nelson "used to have [Winnie] picked up so [she] could watch him at the gym, or at meetings, or at rallies. How charming! . . . [They were] part of the glitz of Orlando, Sophiatown, Thulandiville, the entire network of reef townships."

· · · · ·

"He was a peacock showing off his feathers to a potential mating partner. So handsome. And you, so stunningly beautiful. The glamour of celebrity and the danger of politics came together in an elaborate foreplay of social energy."

*Njabulo Ndebele, from* The Cry of Winnie Mandela *(2003)*

· · · · ·

## *Drum* Magazine: Sophiatown's Voice

The most memorable record of the "fabulous decade," as writer Lewis Nkosi dubbed it, was imprinted in *Drum* magazine, a tabloid-style paper for Africans established in 1951. It was in these pages that the Sophiatown generation of "detribalized African cockneys" found its voice. Though edited and owned by whites, *Drum* made the careers of a host of talented writers including the exposé journalist

Henry Nxumalo ("Mr. Drum"), Nat Nakasa, Bloke Modisane, Can Themba, Nkosi himself. On its showbiz pages as in its reportage, in its sports journalism as in its finely-styled short stories, the *Drum* writers captured the characteristic tone of Sophiatown, a vigorous, slangy "jazz speak."

Appealing to a continental, Pan-African readership, *Drum* communicated both at a higher-brow, literary level and, more usually, through a semiliterate picture language featuring boxers, beauty queens, social workers, respectable family patriarchs—pictures that represented role models for the target black bourgeois audience. Significantly, Nelson and Winnie Mandela taken together as a couple embodied among the most prominent of these roles. Mandela, pictured in a good suit at the Treason Trial, was in fact a 1956 *Drum* "cover boy." His showcasing as the archetypal African cosmopolitan and bespoke nationalist politician is therefore to a degree attributable to the efforts of the talented and also widely accessible *Drum* generation of writers. From the standpoint of this literary community as aware of the importance of self-presentation as of self-representation, of black style as of black pride, the smart politician with the film-star smile appeared as a *definitive leader* in so far as he was *also* an unparalleled *urban sophisticate*.

Reflecting on the historical moment of *Drum*, the writer Ezekiel Mphahlehle once said: we "[dig] our feet into an urban culture on impossible terms. . . . Ours is a fugitive culture: borrowing here, incorporating there, retaining this, rejecting that." Tragically, it was also a fugitive culture in that, by the mid-1960s, with Johannesburg's "black spot" removals long completed, its most prominent players were on the run, in jail or in exile. Today, the sad demise of the fabulous

*Drum* generation of artists polishes its glamorous image by contrast, and gives the 1950s Mandela, the man about Sophiatown, the air of a figure from another age. Yet the concept of an impossible, fugitive black culture is important, too, for what it says about the symbolic struggle that urban life represented for self-consciously modern Africans. Like the lawyers Tambo and Mandela, like the shebeen trumpeters and crooners, *Drum*'s writers worked with a live sense of creating *against the odds* conditions of self-determination for the black urban community.

Apartheid was not merely an institutional order but, in the words of critic Leon de Kock, "a condition of being . . . a predicament," which meant that for urban Africans to enter official history (history with a capital "H"), they had willy-nilly to commit a torsion upon it. Recasting European forms in their own terms, they forged a "suture of the incommensurate." With its stories of desperate battles for survival, and transient moments of romance before inevitable loss, *Drum* magazine's pages outline how tough it was for black South Africans to make this historical entry and live this fissured reality, and, moreover, to do so with stylish ease. *Drum* shows what feats of adaptation and ingenuity were required to map a coherent and above all modish path through the apartheid predicament, whether via political resistance like Sophiatown's "We Won't Move" campaign, or in writing itself.

During the years Mandela spent working in the intercultural hurly-burly of central Johannesburg, he developed the dynamism (the quality Sisulu first discerned in him) that allowed him to override the feelings of self-alienation that bruised many of his peers, and to burst into the modern present. As much as from Gandhi's by-1952-historically-distant example, he learned from the visual spectacle that was Sophiatown how to choreograph an image in order to press a political point. In the downtown streets where the flashy personality was encouraged to present the star turn that was himself, he honed the showmanlike confidence that he would use to public effect at Rivonia to give one of the twentieth century's great speeches, and, much later, within the lower-key forum of the nego-tiation table. As we will next see, he here perceived that an assured masculine style could effectively counter the prevailing stereotypes of blacks as backward, rural, and the like. Indeed, he had by 1962 become so forward as an *agent of history*, a self-conscious political operator within and between communities, that he liked to phone journalists to report on his own movements underground.

Mandela's capacity for self-projection despite apartheid repression is explored in the next chapter, which foregrounds the ANC leader as a turbocharged, always intensely masculine performer. Yet not only his mask-wearing and shape-shifting, but also, a related quality, his rela-tive freedom from dogma, can be explained by the fact that his political education took place within the very crucible of South African jazz. Only with difficulty could his sensibilities have escaped the atmo-sphere of risk and improvisation, of extravagant borrowing and free-wheeling style that characterized Johannesburg's mixed dance halls and music clubs. His political practice ever since, it can be argued, has been noticeably marked by the rhythms and syncopations of Fordsburg and Sophiatown's music, its contrapuntal interminglings and offbeat tangents. Throughout his career, he has often interested himself in pursuing an *experimental line* (in novelist J. M. Coetzee's phrase) in contradistinction to his party's line. He advocated violence when other ANC leaders were sticking to passive resistance. In prison he built rapport with the enemy. And even if the response was belated, he promoted HIV/AIDS awareness when the South African state's policy was to deny the existence of AIDS.

# SIX

## Masculine Performer

•

AT HIS TRIALS IN BOTH 1962 AND 1964 Mandela chose, after consultation, to *represent himself* in the dock, thinking that the direct form of address this afforded him would create an ideal opportunity for broadcasting the political vision of the already-banned ANC. In this he was massively successful. His two strategically planned and rhetorically patterned speeches propelled the African nationalists' anti-apartheid fight in South Africa on to the world stage, and, moreover, shone the historical limelight centrally on Mandela.

In any memoir involving the ANC leader, this is the keynote that is repeatedly struck: his chameleonlike talent for donning different guises; his theatrical flair for costume and gesture; his shrewd awareness of the power of his own image. Across his career he played such various roles

This photo was taken during a 1994 election rally in Gauteng province—symbolically significant as the site of the 1960 Sharpeville Massacre—after supporters had presented Mandela with a gift of African-style clothing.

as counselor, lawyer, showman, guerrilla leader, and statesman, and allowed himself profligately to be photographed in these guises. As was seen, he delighted in acting the *shape-shifter*, assuming a range of contrasting masks and mien, and convincing others of their authenticity. His city persona, for example, expressed a modern yet unmistakably African nationalist self-assurance: *this*, his look proclaimed, was the style of the coming African man, the citizen of the future.

On the run in 1961–2, he positively thrived in the costumes his life-in-hiding necessitated, and the sense of theater and risk of exposure involved in wearing them. Not for nothing was he called the Black Pimpernel, after the protagonist of Baroness Orczy's well-loved 1905 novel *The Scarlet Pimpernel*, an aristocratic English master of ingenious disguises at the time of the French Terror. He is said not to have resented the appellation. It appealed to his sense of himself as able to establish rapport with a variety of different audiences—"with Muslims in the Cape . . . sugar workers in Natal . . . factory workers in Port Elizabeth," he writes in his autobiography. It appealed also to his desire for mastery of any situation in which he might find himself: a feature that *Long Walk to Freedom* does not openly address.

This chapter highlights Nelson Mandela's breathtaking abilities as a performer and manipulator of images—qualities central to an understanding of his historical achievement, and of how this intercalated with the ANC's political vision. From the late 1950s, especially after the controversial shift to violence, it is clear that his organization, despite its emphasis on the collective, tirelessly worked to exploit his self-projection as a symbolic man of destiny. For an exiled movement in need of messianic leadership, Mandela fitted the bill perfectly and, indeed, was happy to style his image so as to advance the nationalist cause.

It is this that accounts for the choreographed quality that any account of his life inevitably carries: his performances were composed with a remarkable degree of self-knowledge. He was never unaware of the power of making a physical statement; of the efficacy, whether in public or private, of masks; of how his life might be read as a model for African upward mobility and political success. Even on the 1994 campaign trail, when his reputation was relatively secure, he was famous for addressing a number of People's Forums in one day, changing several times to suit his different audiences (a woolly sweater for a talk to older people, an open shirt for a village crowd). As Mhlaba once remarked, Mandela from the late 1950s was groomed to be the internal ANC leader (the counterpart to Tambo in exile), and "he himself of course conducted himself to attain that status."

Mandela's mastery of performance, though often taken as a given, is rarely, however, analyzed in any depth. This is probably due to the association of such theatricality with charges of changeability and moral hollowness. Yet his capacity for working his image as if it were itself an expression of his politics tells us a great deal not only about his shrewd ability to manipulate his own myth. It also reflects on his proverbial dynamism: how he transformed his *style of activism* into a *credo for action*. It relays his understanding, which he shares with Gandhi, that method and medium are central to politics; that principle is most effectively conveyed through display. Political success to a great extent means transmitting a more humanly convincing message than does one's rival: Mandela shows that he keenly embraces this precept. This in itself would be a strong reason for examining his capacity as a consummate player of roles.

Mandela's awareness of his iconic status can appear cynical, even cunningly postmodern, but at the time it would most accurately have been described as expedient. He saw, as Nehru too saw, that it was important to stand as a "symbolic expression of the confused desires of his people": that embattled anticolonial nationalist movements required compelling unifying images. A reader of Nehru's life-writing, Mandela in his own autobiography fifty years later constructs his life on the assumption that the national leader's story is interlocked with the nation's story, specifically for him the story of anti-apartheid resistance. In his view, the leader, the first democratic president-to-be, *embodies* the nation. Significantly, during his later years in office, Mandela often came across in ways that suggested a self entirely bound up in a public mask, as his co-biographer Richard Stengel commented.

Another strong reason for an analysis of the performer-president is that Mandela in role—*unlike* that other anticolonial arch-performer Gandhi—chose always to act the man, or in ways that reinforced or enhanced his masculinity. If his iconography to some extent embodied his politics, it was a noticeably masculine iconography. To speak of Mandela the man of masks, therefore, allows us to speak also of his projection of a consistently *masterful masculinity*. His play with dress was no effeminate diversion, but a commanding way of presenting himself in the public sphere. Due to a widespread preconception that a nationalist leader has necessarily to be assertive, determined, and hence male, this predominant masculinity is often assumed in studies of Mandela—yet it provided, certainly in the first half of his career, the motor force behind his political authority and moral conduct.

## Sartorial Display

When he entered court for the first time after his high-profile 1962 arrest, Mandela (and Winnie, too) famously chose to wear traditional Xhosa dress, in his case a leopard-skin *kaross*, or robe, to demonstrate that he was carrying on his shoulders his people's historical aspirations. "I felt myself to be the embodiment of African nationalism," he commented. At other times, as we know, he donned smart lawyer's suits to radiate African urban self-confidence—suits that were likewise complemented by Winnie's sophisticated, modern style. His respect for Westminster democracy and gentlemanly values he translated into a liking for the "trappings of British style and manners."

Later, taking the part of Creon in the 1970 Robben Island production of Sophocles' *Antigone*, he said he experienced what it was to be a true lawmaker: the role and the robes gave the feel of reality. By the time of his presidency, his public character seemed to have become one with the infectious smile and air of public bonhomie he had long cultivated. His interactions with the media were almost entirely constituted through the medium of charm, which most were helpless to resist. He artfully combined freedom-fighter celebrity with middle-class respectability, as when he drank tea with Mrs. Verwoerd. He had achieved what one of his cabinet ministers described as a *total politicization of being*.

The predominant aspect of the many eye-catching performances that distinguish Mandela's career is the strong emphasis given to sartorial display: not only acting the part, but also donning the right costume. As for Gandhi, another magus of sartorial semiotics, clothing and style were central to how Mandela projected his different public personas. He worked the vocabulary of dress to assert his control over a situation and to encapsulate the values he espoused. By sharp contrast, his speeches as a rule were unremarkable. Striking mainly in their lack of fluency, they were characterized by an overuse of the set-piece motifs of struggle rhetoric, a fondness for cliché (as of human life as a brief flash upon a stage), and a stiff, admonishing tone (at times not unlike his white counterpart P. W. Botha).

Mandela's heavy-handed rhetorical formality connected also to the relative *invisibility* of the physical and emotive *body* in his speeches. In strange contradistinction to his imposing stature, matters concerning bodily involvement, including sexuality or any form of kinesthetic, are curiously recessive or expressed with extreme modesty. This is an area of noticeable difference from Gandhi, who was unstinting in the projection of his semi-attired physical (if ascetic) body the better to signify his politics.

In Mandela's case, then, clothes most definitely make the man and the politician: dress transmits the moral example—and the model of style—which he seeks to represent on almost every platform he occupies. For him, the most significant political moments are captured in some appropriate costume, to the extent that in certain instances, as in his wearing the traditional green-and-gold Springbok rugby shirt and cap at South Africa's 1995 World Cup victory, the costume *created* the moment. On that July day, he knowingly played both with the standard signifiers of white South African masculinity, and with the elasticity of his own media image. Far from baulking at the cringe-worthy commonplaces with which the event was loaded, as novelist J. M. Coetzee remarks, Mandela embraced them, assisted in this by the well-known fact of the Springbok captain's relative political sensitivity. Though the performance appeared dangerously compromising to many observers, he sought to embody thereby the principle of reconciliation with Afrikanerdom.

In ways uncannily similar to those maverick imperial heroes General Gordon, theatrical Baden-Powell, or indeed Lord Nelson himself—who too might have taken Henley's "Invictus" as their inspiration—Mandela reveled in a sense of public occasion, its combination of formality and drama, convention and improvisation. He enjoyed mastering a situation through sheer verve, guts, and willpower. Like the heroes of empire, he demonstrated a strong sense of historical destiny, understanding that the conviction of being appointed to a task, coupled with an aptitude for theatricality, were central to authoritative leadership. If in later years, as he ever more closely approximated his own myth as secular saint, he sacrificed the trickster qualities of his previous incarnations—the young joker, the Pimpernel-on-the-run—his costumes continued to remind audiences of his wayward humor and unflagging pleasure in casting a pose.

## Embodiment of the Law

From the time of his entry on to a wider political stage with the Defiance Campaign, Mandela was aware not only that the leader's political prospectus should encapsulate his people's aspirations, but also that his physical presence in performance could be seen to configure the nation's dreams. In his law practice with Tambo, established that same year, Mandela quickly built a reputation as an assertive advocate, cultivating a theatrical manner in court which contrasted with his partner's more retiring approach. He saw that his profession as a black lawyer working amid the contradictions of apartheid society demanded this dramatic boldness, indispensable armor in a context where black men were routinely humiliated.

But his performances also shrewdly invoked the values that underlay his professional success: the patrimonial loyalties to community reinforced by the Victorian principle of self-help; the English etiquette instilled by his mission education; his respect for reasoned debate and the rule of law. *See!* his court appearances announced, here is a black man outdoing the white at representing the very civilized values that he, the white man, would deny me. The impact was supremely subversive, precisely because in making his claims, Mandela was incarnating the principles of law and liberty that white authority attached exclusively to itself.

By the time of his trial for sabotage in 1962, Mandela was more aware than most that the space of the court could be used as a political theater. It was a place unconstrained like no other in the country by the discriminatory restrictions imposed on Africans. His 1964 speech from the dock with its step-by-step exposition of the ANC's history and turn to armed violence, demonstrated a keen awareness of historical moment and audience, and of the sheer freedom that the opportunity to expound afforded.

Throughout the speech, Mandela finely balances his different allegiances—to tradition and modernity, to nationalism and communism, to the West and Africa. He is conscious that each measured word both delivers an exposé of the injustices black South Africans have suffered, and, even more powerfully, dramatizes the *black commitment to justice* in contrast with the "banditry" of white law (Bloke Modisane's memorable phrase). He gives authoritative witness to—he enacts, he *is*—black integrity and capability here, now, within South Africa. The French philosopher Jacques Derrida memorably evoked Mandela's invocation of the pure spirit of the law in a 1986 essay. Appealing over the heads of his judges, representatives of a debased law, Derrida wrote, Mandela stood for a higher justice. "[Setting] himself against the code within the code," he became the ultimate expression of the rationalist legal traditions associated with the Enlightenment.

In prison, deprived of the underpinnings of authority provided by public stage and appropriate dress, Mandela developed other methods of asserting his vision and will, which again, however, involved bold self-projection, if in more intimate surroundings. It was entirely predictable that the first complaint he lodged targeted the demeaning short trousers African prisoners were forced to wear. At issue, yet again, was the way in which dress configured personal and political dignity. In the confined corners of cell and exercise yard, he also explored the possibilities of a different type of discourse. The fiery guerrilla leader modulated per force into the low-profile interlocutor who, however, his eye still on the *look* of any action, often singled out individuals from *other* organizations for conversation. In his interactions with the prison authorities he always remained impeccably correct in his manners, even when provoked. Visitors, announced or unexpected, he addressed with characteristic gravity. Politeness was again a way of demonstrating by contrast African self-control and respect for the law.

Following the 1990 release, when his image once again went public, then, too, Mandela the man worked together with the myth his organization had built to express, in particular, *representativeness*. He vigorously rejected any notion of occupying an elevated position, and spoke of the danger of personality cults in African politics. Yet his brokering between the ANC and the government depended precisely on the authority he bore as an individual leader, his capacity to *speak for* his movement and country, and *to* his people, as his famously liberal use of the collective first person suggested. The many times on which he sued for compromise on the ANC's behalf depended almost entirely on this store of what has been called "moral capital," of acting in ways consistent with certain core principles. On the hustings in 1994 he fully identified himself with his organization's campaign. He signified in his practice and upon his body the prestige he had acquired as a young commander and political prisoner, but also, even more intensively, he encapsulated a prospective new South African identity—liberated, expansive, mobile, inclusive.

It was predictable that this national message would, yet again, be expressed sartorially. In the early to mid-1990s, abandoning his cosmopolitan suits, Mandela took to wearing the relaxed, colorful *Madiba shirts* that became his trademark—and a desirable commodity in South African tourist shops. Far from being authentically African, Indonesian President Suharto had introduced Mandela to these shirts on his 1990 Asian tour. He adopted the loose-fitting but dressy garment not so much for how it harmonized with the concept of the rainbow nation, as might appear, but because of its comfort. Yet, while allowing him to "feel freedom" (his words), the shirt also permitted him to figure an old man's hard-won but still dignified casualness, with ethnic rainbow hues thrown into the mix.

In short, from as far back as 1952, certainly in the years 1990–9, Mandela's public political life can be viewed as an ongoing publicity event, in which he was both the centerpiece and the most relentless of managers. He perceived, as had Gandhi, how crucial the retooling of a charismatic image was in a conflict with an unpredictable adversary. By the time of his retirement, he had transmuted into a virtual logo for his country as well as a sign of himself, as is captured in how his smiling face ubiquitously features on South African tourist industry Web sites.

## Formal Speech

No account of Mandela the showman is complete without giving attention to the curious immobility of his verbal performances: of how the strained, affectless tones that marked his early attempts at public speaking continued, though with some modification, to run as a mode across his career. This stiffness characterized not merely his speeches, but the polemical articles written for publications like *Liberation* (1953–9), and his political-pedagogical statements in prison. How did his seemingly wooden language—his *langue de bois*—coordinate with the versatility of his statesmanlike behavior?

Rhetoric, according to the classic definition, is fundamental to persuasion, as is good delivery to a successful performance. For Mandela, however, persuasion often depended rather on the projection of leaderly authority through highly mechanical forms of address. In "Tamed," written in response to the February 1990 "Release" speech, the poet Tatamkhulu Afrika evocatively describes Mandela both as a godhead raised on an "alienating pedestal, piled for your pinioning," and a mere old man, manipulated by historical forces, fed "stolidly" with words "as into a machine." Across the years, as this implies, Mandela's sartorial language often worked with more eloquent effect than his formal speeches, though his stolidity at the same time underpinned his chiefly demeanor.

Rather than being a master of postapartheid rhetoric, as the critic Philippe-Joseph Salazar suggests, Mandela could instead be said to have deployed the *rhetoric of postapartheid mastery*. This is apparent from that same February 11 speech, drafted together with Cyril Ramaphosa and Trevor Manuel. At this time of the reemergence of the leader-in-waiting, the concern of the speechwriting troika was to assert collective leadership and dispel suspicions regarding his possible collaboration with the enemy. Hence, to the disappointment of listeners around the world, Mandela's bullish devotion throughout the address to long-winded formal and formulaic salutations to the ANC's supporting constituencies. Similar litanies of acknowledgment marked other speeches at the time. (Interestingly, although Mandela worked with several different speechwriters during his career, the humdrum quality of his language remained a constant and so, presumably, a preference.)

It is indicative that Mandela was always a more impressive speaker in court than out of it. The lawyer's bench and the dock granted him a certain license as a crowd-pleaser, where he learned to mold his wooden tones to fit the smooth modulations of a legal argument. Elsewhere, motivated by a strong sense of responsibility to his people, he consistently avoided appearing the demagogue. To encourage support, he used a pared-down, generalist language, the verbs straightforward and workmanlike, the nouns often abstract—invoking freedom, democracy—but unadorned. In all cases, in the dock and on the podium, his reasoned stage-by-stage progressions and set phrases were designed to control the expression of subjective emotion.

Unless on those relatively rare occasions when his anger at an abuse of power expressed as exhortation, Mandela's was a public discourse from which the affect had been extracted. We were not to know how Madiba felt, how Rolihlahla felt. For one as dedicated as he was to achieving consensus through the assertion of agreed-upon principle, it made no sense to amplify or overqualify his words. His repetitive, starkly polarized binaries (dark/light, life/death, African people/white government); the predictable imagery of extensive battles, long walks, and slow upward climbs (made safe by endorsements from Shakespeare and Nehru)—in short, the clichés he so preferred were first and foremost a means of insisting upon concord.

The tension that exists in Mandela between *two modes of leadership*, in biographer Tom Lodge's reading, could be seen as stamped upon his verbal performances, in the contrast between the occasional roused, magisterial tones, on the one hand, and the more deadpan, ministerial delivery, on the other. Inspired by his courtly background, he at times subscribed to traditional notions

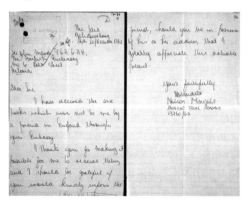

**Mandela's communications often display** a careful formality. This 1962 letter from Mandela to the British embassy was written while he was in prison.

of *consensual decision-making*. This approach was arguably expressed via an authoritative vocabulary of collective identification and occasional reliance on embellishment and mini-allegory, as in his well-known citation of the Ingrid Jonker poem (about the African child bestriding the world) in the May 24, 1994, State of the Nation address. Elsewhere, however, he used the constrained formulas of *liberal self-determination* and *democratic rule*. He revealingly used this kind of telegraphic, empirical language, pitted against the vulgar excesses of the colonial state, in his 1960s justifications of armed resistance. It was this second mode, too, that—to close a circle—provided the strategic foil to his exuberant, individualized performances on the political stage.

## Masculine Madiba

From the time he entered his guardian-the-regent's court, through his legal and political work in Johannesburg, to the prison years, each one of the social-cultural worlds Mandela occupied was organized on patriarchal lines underpinned by masculinist attitudes. Small wonder then that across most of his life he viewed not merely national heroism but historical agency itself strictly in masculine terms. Small wonder, too, that in his supporters' eyes, his assertive, heterosexual masculinity represented the taken-for-granted scaffolding for his charismatic leadership.

In his 1964 court notes made in the event that a death sentence was pronounced, Mandela's pride in his cause was resonantly expressed in the final words, that he would go to meet his fate "like a man." The words unconsciously echoed the cry the initiate Rolihlahla battled to utter at the moment of his circumcision. As for most postcolonial nationalist movements, to be a human subject for Mandela was to be a man. In his autobiography, though published in 1994, the South African liberation struggle is generically described as the "black man's" experience. Here, again, Mandela marks an area of difference from Gandhi. Whereas for Gandhi anticolonial resistance demanded a refusal of the masculinist forms through which Western authority was expressed—an overall feminization of political method—for Mandela, conversely, nationalist self-assertion involved fully coming into one's own as a man—this despite his hospitality to women's modes of protest.

Under empire, as is widely recognized by commentators, gender identities were enlisted in the service of colonial power. Within the colonial hierarchy European authority tended to be cast as masculine (dominant, rational), while social regulations and cultural representations effeminized the colonized, in particular men, the better to effect their subjugation. Significantly, in several letters of complaint written in prison, Mandela referred to the abuses the inmates suffered as *emasculating*. In South Africa, the white union of 1910 had substantially reinforced the discriminatory colonial regime of masculine and feminine value that had operated from the 1700s. Its draconian land and labor laws polarized families along strict gender lines, eventually penning migrant mineworkers in all-male compounds in the cities.

In South Africa, as in other former colonies, therefore, the subversion of imposed gender ideologies became an essential move in the anticolonial game. Prominent figures in the nationalist community felt bound to assert a forceful, overcompensatory masculinity, counterpointed by the elevation of rural mothers as symbols of national virtue. Moreover, in a context in which both mission school and workplace reproduced the traditional family's patriarchal framework, the story of the African's entry into urban modernity became, almost inevitably, a male-dominated story. Although Mandela grew up at a remove from direct colonialism, his Johannesburg worlds were at once colonial and patriarchal in their divisions: here both black nationalists and urban sophisticates resisted discrimination through representing as "manly" men. The projection of a *hypermasculinity*, in theorist Ashis Nandy's memorable phrase—a masculinity that was aggressive, uncompromising, domineering toward women—was the stance that the male African nationalist was under pressure to adopt.

Mandela is on record for having said that it wasn't till the time for reflection his prison years afforded that he began to develop a more critical attitude toward the conventional equation of leadership with masculinity. At the Great Place the young Nelson had, after all, witnessed Jongintaba's authoritarian rule expressed as deliberation between exclusively male chiefs. The "home boy" networks he used to get ahead in Johannesburg played to the advantage of those who stood upon their traditional status. As in Can Themba's *Drum* story "Mob Passion," the cultural spaces of the city—the Bantu Men's Social Club, jazz clubs, the magazine's pages itself—constituted pungently macho worlds, where he found he could thrive precisely by burnishing his easygoing but dynamic masculine persona.

True, as someone impressed by the "intelligent" women students at Fort Hare, Mandela appreciated the fact that his first and second wives were both educated professionals. He recognized that their success represented a significant achievement for black women. Yet, though he sought them out for their modern attitudes, his relationships with Evelyn and Winnie were all the same, the biographies record, characterized by conventional gender expectations. Once his marriage to Evelyn Mase had ended, he presented her with their divorce papers as a *fait accompli*. His courtship of Winnie Madikizela, conducted while he was involved in the Treason Trial, was stage-managed by him: his proposal came in the form of an announcement that her wedding dress had been ordered. As he found underscored in *Drum*, urban modernity involved conformity with the ideals of individualist romantic love and bourgeois domesticity. On Robben Island in 1970, he wrote to Winnie to convey regret at having left her to child-rearing without more considerate help from him.

In the political realm, too, in contradistinction to how African men in white service were addressed as "boys," the ANC, and its Youth League in particular, expressed nationalist aspiration via images of combativeness and virility, while threats to the same, conversely, were seen as affronts to masculinity. Lilian Ngoyi, ANC Women's League President in the 1950s, a lover of Mandela's at the time of the breakup of his first marriage, was interestingly represented in *Drum* both as a fearsome ball-breaker and, at the same time, as soft inside, confirming gender dichotomies. Mandela himself, self-reliant from an early age, comfortable with the gravitas of status, used to assuming a lordly air, was able to project an overtly masculine identity relatively effortlessly, if also self-consciously. In his aggressive heckling at meetings, as in his gentlemanly court demeanor, he conducted himself so as to reinforce an indubitable African *and* masculine authority.

His assured role-play was also prominently on show in his relaxed friendships with white women like Helen Joseph, Ruth First, and Mary Benson associated with the Congress of Democrats and the ANC—friendships that his male biographers describe as remarkable (though they were all haute-bourgeois ladies). In many anticolonial contexts it has been the case that the nationalist hero's masculinity is heightened through his connection with an allegedly prized white femininity. Such connection represented not merely the desire for the sexually forbidden—the more obvious explanation—but a yearning for less uneven gender relations than were generally possible with black women, given colonial hierarchies. For

Mandela, it is clear, these friendships were fueled by an intellectual plea-sure in meeting with women, of whatever race, on an equal footing as fellow activists. With Helen Joseph, for example, he felt sufficiently at ease to talk about his initiation while en route to the Treason Trial in her car. He forged lasting contacts, too, with the wives of his Indian Congress colleagues, like Amina Cachalia, who inducted him into the pleasures of their cooking. In his autobiography he discusses gravitating to women, as with them he could "confess to weaknesses and fears I could never reveal to another man": he was free to act as less dominantly masculine. In their turn, these women, without exception, felt charmed by his politeness, trademark smile, and impressive physique.

Yet if Mandela's masculinist, heterosexual role-play consistently formed an expression of his nationalist politics, it was not engaged without tension, as was brought out in particular by his thoughtful, eclectic reading in prison. One of the first women writers he ever encountered, his "precious girl" Nadine Gordimer, especially her *Burger's Daughter*, took him "beyond visible horizons," he once commented, and changed his perspective on gender roles in the struggle. He now began to write to Winnie in ways that acknowledged their partnership: "With you on my side" he said in 1969, "I always feel part of an invincible force that is ready to win new worlds." Many of his early attitudes toward women had been "totally wrong." He expressed admiration for figures like Margaret Thatcher (her political determination as a woman prime minister, not her politics), and for powerful widows in his own Thembuland lineage.

Mandela's raised gender awareness was confirmed in his partner-ship with his third wife, Graça Machel. The widow of Samora Machel had been for some considerable time an important public figure in her own right in her native Mozambique. With her marriage to Mandela she arguably extended these roles. Even so, his rejection of his former masculinist preconceptions did not diminish his delight in posing alongside the range of media and fashion beauties he entertained in his postprison years (Princess Diana, the Spice Girls, Oprah Winfrey, Charlize Theron). Yet his charmed collusion in the media objectification of these women is arguably tempered by his willingness to stand alongside them as a pinup, and, more generally, offer himself as a shining figurehead for various causes: the HIV/AIDS awareness campaign; his own Children's Fund.

Mandela's robust masculinity has always assumed a largely *unexamined heterosexuality* as its foundation, though here again there are points of ambivalence. In prison he appears to have overlooked homosexual occurrences, on the grounds first of alleged ignorance, and, once disabused of this, of disgust, though he was willing to admit in principle that such "unnatural" acts might take place. Years later, however, when he belatedly espoused the HIV/AIDS campaign, he made the controversial acknowledgment that this "Western" "gay disease" had become an African disease also: it was important, he felt, to "break the silence." In prison, too, though he maintained his own silence about his feelings, Mandela was never afraid to show a feminine tenderness and solicitousness toward his friends. This quality emerged especially in his relations with short-statured Eddie Daniels, the member of the Liberal Party's militant offshoot ARM who at times felt marginalized within the Island's B Section. Mandela taught Daniels the to-him-heartening lines of "Invictus," and personally assisted him with emptying his chamber pot when he was ill. Occasionally he revealed to him the emotional pain imposed by his regime of self-control.

· · · · ·

"I have been fairly successful in putting on a mask behind which I have pined for the family, alone, never rushing for the post when it comes until somebody calls out my name. I also never linger after visits although sometimes the urge to do so becomes quite terrible. I am struggling to suppress my emotions as I write this letter. I have received only one letter since you were detained, that one dated August 22. I do not know anything about family affairs, such as payment of rent, telephone bills, care of children and their expenses, whether you will get a job when released. As long as I don't hear from you, I will remain worried and dry like a desert. I recall the Karoo I crossed on several occasions. I saw the desert again in Botswana on my way to and from Africa—endless pits of sand and not a drop of water. I have not had a letter from you. I feel dry like the desert. Letters from you and the family are like the arrival of summer rains and spring that liven my life and make it enjoyable. Whenever I write to you I feel that inside physical warmth, that makes me forget all my problems. I become full of love."

*Nelson Mandela, from a letter to Winnie Mandela (October 1976)*

· · · · ·

## Neolitha's Body

The contusion in Mandela of exuberant performance and suppressed feeling points to the possibility that his dazzling masculine act, including as a debonair president receiving celebrities, itself involved a studious repression of the sensory body. Did his Teflon masculinity constitute one of the primary defenses making up his protective social shield? Certainly those appearances with female icons from the worlds of entertainment and charity showbiz involved extravagant acts featuring theatrical flattery and scripted lines—acts which became ever more repetitive and superficial the more the president spoke of himself in private as the "loneliest man." Was his masculine role-play, as this suggests, caught up in the masks he was so good at maintaining, rather than with the feeling human being? And might the self-control, to which this successful masculine front was bolted, connect with that remarkable *absence* of the *corporeal body* from his public speeches, even his talks about HIV/AIDS?

The child who from an early age learned to exercise extreme self-discipline, Mandela always exhibited an "aversion to personal discussion." Expressions of vulnerability he confined to letters, as in his 1976 letter to Winnie about wearing protective masks (above). Emotional crises, whether of desire or sorrow, were contained behind his many convincing masculine shows: indeed, his mask appeared to *emerge from* his negation of his potentially weak, "feminine" body. To Mandela, the body was altogether too chaotic an entity to admit into the masculine domain of nationalist politics, even when this was limited to the prison yard.

This is one possible explanation, yet it requires support from another, based in an understanding of the forms of bodily repression and Victorian-type modesty that characterized the colonial/apartheid system. To be sure, Mandela did not entirely deny his desires: in sport and in his relationships with women he took a warm if covert pleasure in the kinesthetic, erotic body. A prominent sign of this pleasure, a *National Geographic* photograph of a bare-breasted, prancing Andaman Islander, whom he called Neolitha, stood for years on his desk in his Robben Island cell in order, he said, to make Winnie "jealous." When in the mornings he dusted Winnie's picture, standing alongside this one, and pressed his nose to hers in the photo as he once had done in reality, he

"[I]n the quietness of the day's dawning, [Mandela] told another story. He told us how one day when he had gone to hug his grown-up daughter she had flinched away from him, and burst out, 'You are the father to all our people, but you have never had the time to be a father to me. . . .' There it was—the one against the other: their work, our needs, their commitments, our lives, there was no squaring the circle. They knew it, somewhere, all their generation: as the state had poured out its wrath, they had watched their children suffer. And yet, and yet—what else could they have done?"

*Gillian Slovo, on the death of her father, Joe Slovo, in*
Every Secret Thing: My Family, My Country *(1997)*

would feel again "the electric current that used to flush through my blood" (see page 153).

Frantz Fanon broke important theoretical ground in the 1950s when in *Black Skin, White Masks* he observed that colonial governance operated through the control and management of bodies: the representation of the colonized as all body—brute, animalistic, savage—was central to colonialism's structure of values. Apartheid, a particularly acute form of colonial oppression, went so far as to declare the black body expendable, acting upon it with extreme violence. As the philosopher Achille Mbembe observes, extending Fanon's reading, colonial mastery required the absolute denial of the other human being: brutality defined the horizons of colonized existence. From this it followed, he contends, that resistance was most powerfully achieved, and liberation effected, when the colonized denied themselves, their own bodies, and brought themselves into confrontation with death—as of course did Mandela in the conclusion to his Rivonia Trial speech. Otherwise put, if the current conditions of life were inimical to freedom, winning freedom had to involve overcoming or canceling life itself.

This perception illuminates Mandela's abiding interest in two moments in Shakespeare when death is described as implacable. It may also illuminate the forcefulness with which ideals like freedom and justice are asserted in his prose. In *Julius Caesar* II.ii, Caesar invokes death as "a necessary end" that "will come when it will come." This passage Mandela autographed as his favorite in Sonny Venkatrathnam's *Collected Shakespeare*, acknowledging that these were words that encompassed his acceptance of the authority of death. Yet his sense of a person's death as following a script as much as does their life is even more clearly evoked in the lines from *Measure for Measure* III.i, in which the Duke instructs Claudio, "Be absolute for death." These were lines that Mandela pondered while awaiting the Rivonia sentence, and, indeed, Claudio's words to the Duke directly preceding this command had already appeared as the resounding conclusion to his court speech: "But if needs be, it is an ideal for which *I am prepared to die*."

Counterpointing the authority granted to death, an equally important element in the historical process of black liberation struggle was the effort to *recover the self*—an effort that can also be read into Mandela's concern to safeguard his emotional being. His public discourse confronts the hostility to the black body of the apartheid system by choosing, strategically if defensively, to absent that body, to give way to an apparently excessive modesty. He resists the colonial obsession with the oppressed's so-called corporeality by neatly removing the African body, indeed all bodies, from consideration, asserting an ethical stance instead.

His determination in doing so was no doubt facilitated by his never having been physically tortured while in prison, yet it is no less uncompromising for all that. His autobiographical language, too, is noticeably free of physical and emotional preoccupations. His is strictly nonconfessional, denotative prose, and as such it contrasts even with the writing of his model, the always professional, emotionally costive Nehru.

Mandela absorbed apartheid's impact on the body of the oppressed by, in effect, embracing its negations, as exemplified in the punishing regime to which he subjected himself from an early age, in prison as at school. The Mandela body may have been full of style, but it was also always disciplined. On Robben Island he rose every day at 3:30 a.m. for two hours of exercise. At Victor Verster and thereafter his schedule remained almost unchanged. In as much as the colonial state operated through forcing individual bodies to internalize its rules, Mandela effectively outdid it at that process of internalization. As the next chapter shows, he survived stringent circumstances by excelling at stringency.

• • • • •

"Your beautiful photo still stands about two feet above my left shoulder as I write this note. I dust it carefully every morning for doing so gives me the pleasant feeling that I'm caressing you as in the old days. I even touch your nose with mine to recapture the electric current that used to flush through my blood whenever I did so. Neolitha stands on the table directly opposite me. How can my spirits ever be down when I enjoy the fond attention of such wonderful ladies?"

*Nelson Mandela, from a letter to Winnie Mandela (May 1979)*

• • • • •

# SEVEN

## Specters in the Prison Garden

•

THREE IMAGES from the spectral island garden:

Working in the prison's blinding-white lime quarry Mandela and his fellow prisoners were by the day's end covered in a layer of snowy dust. To one another they appeared as ghosts.

Over a decade's digging in this same quarry damaged Mandela's eyes, as it did his comrades'. In his case the damage blocked his tear ducts, which meant he could not cry tears. His tears, even at times of sorrow, were invisible tears—phantom tears.

Until the early 1980s visits from Mandela's family, including Winnie, were strictly "noncontact." In a letter to his daughter Zindzi, in which he mentioned her paying a visit to Cape Town, he suggested she look across Table Bay to Robben Island and imagine him there. This act

**During his imprisonment on Robben Island,** off the coast of Cape Town, South Africa, Mandela took up drawing as one way to come to terms with the bleakness of his surroundings. This colorful depiction of the interior of his cell is one of five in a series called "My Robben Island."

of projection was one that many of his fellow South Africans indulged in through his eighteen years of offshore incarceration, during which almost no photographs of the island inmates were released into the public domain. To his dear ones as to the nation at large, Prisoner 466/64, the inmate of Cell No. 5, became in effect a bodiless, intangible presence: a specter, a ghost.

· · · · ·

"Between 1964 and 1990 he was absented from the political present, yet remained a preeminent inhabitant of South Africa's past and future. He lived on the cusp of time, embodying a people's hope, yet monumentalized on a scale ordinarily reserved for the dead."

*Rob Nixon, from* Homelands, Harlem, and Hollywood *(1994)*

· · · · ·

Following the portrait of Mandela the flamboyant performer, this chapter considers his prison years 1962–90, chiefly the time in Robben Island Maximum Security Prison, but also in Pollsmoor and Victor Verster, a period abruptly separated from the vital 1950s, yet as significant to his formation. Mandela, it is important to remember, was incarcerated for a longer period than his political mentors Gandhi and Nehru—though they were imprisoned more frequently. And his time in prison was itself characterized by sharply contrastive features, which group into three clusters.

First, there were the predominant *spectral qualities* of life on the island, as intimated, which include the at-first-almost-dreamlike instances of cooperation between prisoners and warders, counterweighed by, second, the rigid, often *brutal regime* of everyday existence. Third, there were the important *transformative aspects* of the incarceration, which emerge from this combination of rough physicality and the ghostly-though-human. These aspects are bound up in the activity of gardening, of drawing life, color, hope, and sustenance out of dirt, which was so important to Mandela throughout his twenty-seven and a half prison years. Gardening, as it turned out, offered him a practical correlative to his visions of change. He learned through cultivation to give concrete form to his dreams (and in this resembled many other dispossessed, according to theorist Hélène Cixous).

At the time Mandela entered prison he was a hotheaded, opinionated young leader, given to pedantry, full of derivative ideas—as he himself reflected in a June 20, 1970, letter to his wife. He emerged from these secluded years reflective, disciplined, able to force a consensus and yet to draw the humanity out of another by sheer conviction and persistence. What was the chemistry of the otherworldly and the down-to-earth that brought about this change? For it was by no means a foregone conclusion that Mandela would step out of prison as he eventually appeared: dignified, thoughtful, exceptionally free from bitterness, secure in the knowledge that, as he said, "a simple exposition of principles" sheds light on "universal truths."

· · · · ·

"Besides clothes, bedding, and our ballies [chamber pots], we had nothing else in our cells. We had to observe strict silence in our section. At weekends and on public holidays we were locked up for twenty-four hours at a stretch, with thirty minutes of exercise in the morning and another thirty minutes in the afternoon. During the week we would break stones in the yard, or work in the quarry, from 8:00 a.m. to 4:00 p.m. We were locked up at 4:30 p.m. and would have our supper in our cells. By 8:00 p.m. we all had to be asleep. The lights remained on throughout the night and a warder locked in the section with us kept us under observation . . . from the corridor."

Eddie Daniels, from There and Back (1998)

· · · · ·

## Ghosts and the Regime

Robben (Seal) Island, which lies about six miles from the city of Cape Town, washed by treacherous currents, was used as a place of banishment from the time of early Dutch colonization. It carries its full complement of legends of haunting. There is the fearsome *Flying Dutchman* phantom schooner that plies these waters, and the story of the Malayan spiritual leader, the Prince of Madura, who died here (whose shrine stands nearby the prison). There is the drowned nun who is seen when the fog lies heavy around the Cape of Storms. The first to be exiled to the island was the Khoi interpreter (and only successful escapee) Autshumao in 1658. During the devastating nineteenth-century Xhosa land wars, the British authorities confined rebels here including Mandela's ancestor Chief Makana. Already marked as a dumping ground for society's excluded, the island housed a leper colony and a lunatic asylum between 1844 and 1913. Twenty-nine ships have been wrecked off its shores.

Today the "World Heritage" Robben Island complex, the small town, leper graveyard, and the two main blocks of prison buildings (once separating common-law from political prisoners), has

**Robben Island, site of the former prison** where Mandela spent eighteen of his twenty-seven years of incarceration, has been a museum since 1997 and a UNESCO World Heritage Site since 1999. It is also a center of natural conservation. This photograph of Robben Island was shot from nearby Table Mountain.

the drably everyday aspect of other former places of incarceration and suffering: Dachau and Auschwitz, the West African slave forts. Yet although unthreatening, even old-fashioned, in appearance, this place, no one can forget, was once experienced as a claustrophobic hell. It was without comfort, without contact with the outside world, seemingly without hope, as the prison memoirs of Neville Alexander and Ahmed Kathrada, among others, describe, and Fugard, Kani, and Ntshona's striking play *The Island* (1974) still strongly evokes.

During their time in this place of pariahs, shut out of history, Mandela and his comrades became to all intents and purposes *living ghosts*—to borrow a definition (used in another context) from Jacques Derrida's *Specters of Marx*. Up until the 1980s' Free Mandela Campaign, they were from the viewpoint of their country "not present, nor presently living." Likewise, to them their country and its people had been turned into distant presences whom they would in all likelihood never see again, and certainly not touch, not in the form to which they had bid farewell: they were sentenced *for life*. They populated the past and invoked visions of the future, but the present was not theirs.

As the repressive 1960s wore on, the news blackout in South Africa was so entire that, historian Thomas Karis writes, the ANC organization, in disarray, became a mere "shadowy presence." The government "wanted us to be forgotten by the outside world," island inmate Eddie Daniels remembers. In the refrain of Ghanaian Abena Busia's 1990 poem of homage, "Testament for the First Accused," the ANC leader, "still alive," "still not free," subsists invisibly on the island while on the world stage major events in Pan-African history take place—Martin Luther King's death, Mozambique's independence.

Thick walls separate the individual cells of Robben Island's Section B beside its concrete courtyard where leadership prisoners like Mandela were held. When prisoners were locked up at 4:30 p.m. each day, communication between the cells was virtually impossible. Until the mid-1970s, when the bedding was improved, they would lay themselves to sleep on two stiff blankets and a sisal mat. Many lived in dread of weekends, which were times of near-total isolation. Other political prisoners were held in large, crowded dormitories within the same block and, unlike the "elite" prisoners, were exposed to arbitrary assaults by common-law inmates as well as warders. The food was universally poor: for Africans mainly maize porridge and a watery yeast drink. If the prisoners expressed grievances about the food, as in their favored form of the hunger strike, they were assaulted. In 1965 the prisoners were moved from stone breaking in the courtyard to work chipping lime. For the next fourteen years this activity took up every working day.

Many prisoners unsurprisingly felt beset by a sense of *disorientation* and *disembodiedness*, of being evacuated from society and history: in short, of being reduced to specters. They not only spent long periods in silence, they also were deprived of watches, the most basic facility of self-regulation. Removed from the rest of the world's clock time, they were obliged to give themselves up to the prison system's time regime, controlled by sirens and whistles, the half-hourly counting of the inmates, and the ever-burning lightbulb. Until 1979 they were denied access to news or newspapers, another important medium through which a community understands itself in relation to the unfolding of history. Many filched papers from warders, memorized the news and transferred it verbally, or bartered tobacco for papers with common-law inmates, though they were severely punished if discovered.

D-category prisoners, the classificatory designation at which the Rivonia trialists began their time, were allowed one letter and one family visit every six months. Letters were arbitrarily censored and diaries, too, were confiscated. A third of the first draft of Mandela's autobiography—written at night from 1975 to 1976 at a rate of ten pages a day, copied by Maharaj and Chiba in minuscule handwriting—was discovered buried in document containers in the courtyard garden and confiscated. His "life" was quite concretely taken from him—though the bulk of it appropriately remained hidden in the garden. (The smuggled copy, though it reached England, was not published.) As for visits, the thick glass partition through which visitor faced prisoner made physical contact impossible. Family members spoke to one another strictly in English, via a telephone system with a warder listening on a third handset.

Even though the Island High Command maintained contact with the exiled ANC by way of secret messages, crucial events on the mainland, like the Soweto uprising, were first communicated to the prisoners by means of curious omissions in their routine or unexplained punishments. In this respect, once again, they felt removed from history. For example, on June 16, 1976, the day of the uprising, their supply of hot water was inexplicably cut off. From this alone they were able to deduce that something momentous had taken place. Mandela wrote to Winnie: "Sometimes I feel like one who is on the sidelines . . . who has missed life itself."

An inextricable part of this phantomlike existence was that memory grew acute, as many reported. Images of the past cropped up as if alive. "Here the past literally rushes to memory and there is plenty of time for reflection," Mandela commented. There was a prevalent feeling that people far away were in fact present, which made dreams vivid and often painful. From 1976 Mandela was beset by a recurring anxiety nightmare in which he returned to his old house at 8115 Ngakane Street, Orlando, to find the place deserted. "Finally I would see my home, but it turned out to be empty, a ghost house, with all the doors and windows open but no one there at all." The nightmare was uncannily prescient: the house was gutted by fire in 1988, the piece of wedding cake Winnie had saved for Nelson's return lost. And once he did finally return to his longed-for house, it was to realize in a matter of weeks that his marriage was irretrievably over: his dream image had been an uncanny haunting.

In the early years prisoners were not permitted to speak with one another while working in the quarry, yet, with time, these regulations were relaxed. The change was largely a consequence of persistent prisoner complaints as, seasoned political campaigners, the Section B inmates in particular did not scruple to lodge grievances. In the silence of their cells they self-consciously learned how much was to be gained in terms of both moral and pedagogical support from *structured dialogue*, especially with fellow inmates. From the mid-1960s, study privileges being granted, the more formally educated prisoners began to disseminate economic theory and ANC history to their peers via *sotto voce* tutorials conducted while chipping lime. Although these privileges could be arbitrarily suspended, a kind of *corporate prison life* had by 1969 been established, with regular discussion groups and, on Sundays, board games and sports meets. To "buy" reading time in his cell, Mandela contrived a system of bribing bored night warders with copies of the women's housekeeping magazine *Huisgenoot* (to which his Afrikaans studies entitled him).

A mission-school product, Mandela appears to have found he could most successfully survive Robben Island's rigors by *internalizing* them. Among his fellow inmates he was well known for having effected this internalization with near-total success, bar the few times he registered personal bereavement or insult. Into this internalization—what Wole Soyinka calls his "logic"—it is possible to read the classic response of the child separated early from their home environment: the cultivation of an inner steeliness became a crucial survival mechanism, which, in prison, Mandela deployed with conviction. His inmate colleagues, including close friends like Kathrada, remarked on his growing aloofness and impenetrability across the island years: how he channeled his anger into intellectual argument; how he watched the prison authorities like a hawk. If as a student he had embraced the Victorian work ethic, and if as a lawyer-in-training he had virtually recreated himself through self-discipline (as in the ninety-minute gym routines), he now sought to *embody* steeliness.

Only occasionally, especially when brooding on family relationships in letters home, did he confess to finding an insufficiency of the "steel" he required. To family friend Frieda Matthews he spoke of the "thousand wounds" a man might carry in his heart. Eddie Daniels observed how he sometimes wrapped himself tight in a blanket, as if to cauterize an inner pain. With trusted friends like Daniels he liked to quote as a correlative for his survival-by-rigor his staple "Invictus." Among the other products of imperialist-amputee Henley's pen is the jingoistic collection *For England's Sake*, published to whip up British fervor for the Boer War. Yet in "Invictus," taken on its own, Mandela clearly found his Victorian ethic of self-mastery given compelling expression within the frame of a controlled rhyme scheme supported by strong, monosyllabic nouns. It was only a small step from espousing this poem to assuming a Victorian persona, as he could do in letters to his children. In ways they predictably found alienating, he liked to exhort them to ever-greater effort, reiterating that ambition and drive were the only means of escaping an "inferior position" in life.

However, as many of the prisoners found, it was within this formidably abstracted yet also disciplined environment, far more than in the political hurly-burly of Soweto, that ideas might be held up for sustained inspection and thoroughly analyzed, explored through discussion and in the round. It was in relation to their ghostly dimension of mere living-on—Derrida's dimension of the dead and future generations, but also of prisoners-for-life—that concepts of justice and dignity were most clearly to be comprehended, unrestricted by the circumstances of finite, ordinary life. As Mandela himself wrote in a key essay, "National Liberation": "[Here] [o]ne is able to stand back and look at the entire movement from a distance."

Put differently, Robben Island confined Mandela to the *realm of the symbolic*, which earlier he had already learned skillfully to manipulate for the purposes of legal advocacy. Now he found it a medium in which his political intellect could move with special facility, as when he attempted to approach others' perspectives, including his warders', on their own merits, or identified at different levels with both Creon and Antigone in the Island production of Sophocles' eponymous play. Among prisoner friends he was well known for his tendency to meditate on a move in chess for days at a time: his style "deliberate," his strategy "conservative," as he himself admitted. He was noted, too, for the patience with which he pursued discussion with an interlocutor, relying on his capacity for listening and avoiding judgment, corroborating the other speaker's position with occasional remarks, pushing them gradually to concede common ground.

Once, when inducting the SWAPO leader Toivo ja Toivo into how argument worked on the Island, Mandela provocatively advised him to "engage all and sundry in conversation, during which he could make political points." Particularly difficult debates, as between the ANC and PAC or, later, with Black Consciousness adherents, Mandela liked to imagine literally in 3-D, as a drama played out in a theater. This capacity to focus at length, if anything, deepened over the years, as he learned a new sensitivity to others' needs. (In fact, critics have since suggested, from henceforth Mandela was to conclude that most problems, including difficult economic questions postapartheid, could be solved through the careful balancing of different options, as if the problem were an impasse in an Island board game.)

. . . . .

"Signs of the abstraction of the Island prisoners' thought are found in the pristine state of Mandela's law books. Although most of the heavy tomes bear signs of having been read, and are neatly wrapped in protective plastic, Mandela's marginal 'notes' are restricted to the occasional small tick, as if to mark a place in his reading. Though prisoners tended to avoid note making in order not to be censured, it is here as if case law or jurisprudence were being looked at purely in-and-for-itself, in principle, as a code removed from the considerations of state."

*Author's observation on Mandela's law books,*
*Mayibuye-Robben Island Archive (2006)*

. . . . .

As a group, too, the Section B prisoners indulged their pleasure in exploring ideas—of law, democracy, freedom—at almost indefinite length. They found that their regime of enforced silence and proximity pushed them to establishing rules of decorum for confronting their political differences, while the mode of disciplined dialogue they developed imparted a new sense of intellectual authority. Rank-and-file political prisoners assisted the discussion in a special way, by copying out verbatim extracts from history and political science, for dissemination through the wider group (a practice that continued until the last political prisoners left the island). From their position as specters removed from time—family, sex, getting, spending—yet with time on their hands, the prisoners were able to gain perspective, too, on countervailing points of view. Within the unvarying rhythm of the island's days, positions could be endlessly restated, and eventually subtly revised in relation to one another. Recapitulation, because inevitable, was acceptable and clarifying, especially where viewpoints were diametrically opposed.

In a nutshell, their prison situation allowed these intellectually disciplined, politically experienced men to ponder political problems and processes (resistance, negotiation) in detail and from every available angle, literally for years. As Fran Buntman suggests in her study of Robben Island, the prisoners' efforts to set up an orderly political microcosm transformed their incarceration from a reactive, prohibitive experience, into a *productive social contract*. Their methods—the codes of dialogic conduct they established—would prove fundamental to how Mandela arrived at his *negotiating concept* in the mid-1980s.

Essentially, Section B constituted in itself nothing so much as a ready-made seminar group or think tank, a development the apartheid state had not foreseen, certainly not before Mandela's move to Pollsmoor. As well as his Rivonia group of mostly well-educated friends, Mandela was here surrounded by members of the other liberation parties, especially the PAC but also Maoists and Trotskyists, similarly concerned to study the political process, talk about change, and map areas of agreement. As Minister of Justice Kobie Coetsee brusquely conceded: "The real effect [of putting them together on Robben Island] was to build them."

. . . . .

"There is nothing like a long spell in prison to focus your mind, and to bring you to a more sober appreciation of the realities of your society."

*Mandela to the Commonwealth Eminent Persons Group, 1986*

. . . . .

Yet to describe Robben Island's "University" with an accent on structured exchange should not equate with a suggestion that a Socratic concord prevailed at all times. In the 1960s and 1970s, Mandela disagreed vehemently with radical Marxists like Mbeki and Gwala about such questions as the place of nationalism within a socialist struggle, and the merits of violent "seizure" as against negotiation. Especially after 1976, with the arrival of Black Consciousness prisoners, discussion was often extremely heated. Mandela concentrated on talking through ANC differences with the exclusivist BCM with an unwavering commitment, commanding the new prisoners' respect due to his rationalism and understanding for their youthful hotheadedness. In him they saw, as Seth Mazibuko remembered, how the "bright and shiny instrument" of self-discipline might shape a way into the future.

The painstaking deliberations of prison appear to have sharpened the inmates' conviction of their eventual success. A 1981 Justice Department report on Mandela noticed that imprisonment had failed to dent his idealism or undermine his self-belief. He never doubted that the span of his active life would coincide with the timescale of fundamental change. The prison cell's processes of deliberate, empathetic introspection also brought the important insight that apartheid did not represent simply a case of raw colonial repression, but entailed also the defensive nationalist struggle of the Afrikaner *volk* to retain hold of their hard-won power. For the ANC, therefore, it was necessary to tackle this defensiveness head-on. Discussion especially with warders seems to have reinforced Mandela's faith in the advantages of a multipronged resistance movement. In 1981 or 1985, as in 1964, or even 1952, the armed struggle in his view was to be engaged *alongside* mass mobilization. Once newspapers and political histories were made available to him, he was able to learn from the fate of independence movements elsewhere in Africa how difficult it was for an anticolonial movement to institutionalize itself as a political party after independence. Hence the need to make accommodations with the party in power.

Yet dialogic games of position and maneuver were not Mandela's sole distraction from prison routine. As well as the hidden joys of his letters home, there were, later, at Pollsmoor and Victor Verster, the small indulgences provided by friends and warders, like fish cakes and poached eggs for breakfast, and Romany Cream biscuits. He particularly enjoyed the biryanis Kathrada prepared, which recalled the food Indian Congress activists had supplied during his time underground. The presence of nature on the island, too, offered poignant sources of inspiration: the sea views and birds, the strong, sweeping winds. A rare sighting of the night sky, when the prisoners were once allowed into the prison yard after dark, many remembered as revelatory. Finally, there was to Mandela in particular the relief provided by his gardening hobby, in which his propensity for careful deliberation found external expression in the slow processes of working with seeds and soil.

## Transformation in a Garden

In his often-quoted "Your Logic Frightens Me, Mandela," the poet Soyinka imagines the world's most famous political prisoner cultivating patience and honing his idealism by means of the quiet watchfulness demanded of gardeners. He imagines Mandela befriending the small creatures of the earth, watching grass grow, and even biding his time by working crossword puzzles. Soyinka's speculations were prescient: within Robben Island's barrenness, Mandela had begun a garden.

Given how many prison hours were spent in introspective seclusion, gardening became especially important to Mandela, as it has to other political prisoners, as a link with the material world. The activity of working a garden, of keeping in contact with the earth, in many ways

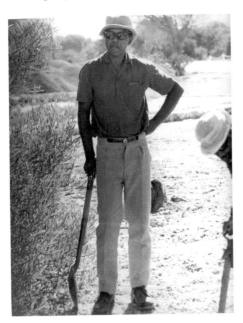

corroborated the processes of regeneration to which he looked forward: as well as relaxation and enjoyment, gardening afforded a readily available correlative for the strategies of political transformation he was sketching in his mind. By giving

**This 1977 photograph** shows Mandela, then a prisoner at Robben Island, tending the garden alongside others in the prison yard.

special consideration to the significance of Mandela's prison gardening, this section examines his alchemy of *freedom through reconstruction* (rather than revolution).

Mandela had acquired some experience of gardening from both his time at Clarkebury Institute and tending the garden at Liliesleaf Farm, Rivonia, where his alias David Motsamayi masked as a gardener. At Clarkebury, he wrote in his autobiography, helping in Reverend Harris's garden not only "planted in me a lifelong love of . . . growing vegetables," but also, importantly, permitted closer human contact than was possible beyond its cooperative parameters: "It helped me get to know the reverend and his family."

Building on these early experiences, Mandela on Robben Island approached the cultivation of a garden in the same way as in 1961–2 he had set out to become a guerrilla fighter: that is, systematically and by the book, "by reading and talking to the experts." Toward the mid-1970s, he and his MK commander Laloo Chiba, known to have green fingers, were granted permission to use as their garden space a strip of opened ground at the far end of the concrete prison yard, at right angles to the Section B corridor. As well as reading any advice manuals he could lay his hands on, Mandela began to measure beds, and weigh and grind compost. The garden was to be productive, not merely decorative: it would grow nutritious vegetables for the prisoners. The prison warders were persuaded to supply seeds (though they were later susceptible to raiding the garden when the prisoners were locked up).

Before long, the prison garden was run as a full-scale operation. By late 1975, Mandela, Chiba, and their helpers had raised two thousand chilies, one thousand tomatoes, and two watermelons, as well as peppers and cucumbers. In a photograph of Mandela's cell taken around this time, ripening tomatoes and peppers are clearly on view, laid out on his desk. Included as the keynote image in the collection of archive photographs, *A Prisoner in the Garden* (2004), the 1977 photograph of Mandela as prison gardener was taken against his will, in a location that was not his garden, yet it, too, stands as an appropriate image of this time. Here we see the political prisoner laying claim to a patch of ground, his island rock, a piece of his nation, by making it fruitful. In the eyes of the world he may be an invisible man, yet in his small garden he is engaged, immediate to himself, fully occupying the present moment.

Despite the at-first unpromising conditions, the shift to the cells on the concrete roof of Pollsmoor Prison interrupted but did not curtail Mandela's gardening activities. Prisoner D220/82 (as 466/64 had now become) undertook to relieve the rooftop's gray monotony by creating a "garden in the sky" using sixteen forty-four-gallon oil drums sawn in half, into which he poured soil carted from the prison's own market garden. Once again, he obsessively watched over the development of the eventual nine hundred plants, helped by his Rivonia colleagues. Once again, warders, including the prison commander, supplied seeds and assisted with erecting hessian barriers against the wind. Echoing the autobiography, prison warder James Gregory observed:

> Eventually, at the height of the growing season, there was a huge variety of plants in the vegetable section: eggplants, cabbage, beans, spinach, carrots, cucumbers, onions, broccoli, lettuce, tomatoes of a number of varieties . . . and many types of spices.

Mandela gave bagfuls of fresh vegetables to the warders, and supplied the kitchen with produce for a "special" Sunday meal. His gardening granted him, he recounts, an almost godlike sense of reshaping the world. "The Bible tells us that gardens preceded gardeners, but that was not the case at Pollsmoor": here he created a "far grander" garden than that at Robben Island.

At his last place of incarceration, as was fitting, a garden was laid on for Mandela's sole use. His deputy governor's cottage at Victor Verster came with an established "idyllic" garden to care for, though its wall was raised to screen his activities from passersby. Even on the day of his release, he took time to show his family and friends the vegetables and now also flowers he had cultivated.

How do we explain the sustained importance of gardening to the prisoner Mandela? For one, from the perspective of a self-styled "country boy," the pleasures of working the earth no doubt recalled the rural environment of his childhood, evoked in nostalgic terms in his letters. For another, in his garden he could practice prudence, self-sufficiency, and provident planning. The etymology of the word *husbandry* signifies both farming and "resourceful management" (*OED*)—specifically, in Mandela's terms, building cooperation and an independent life out of unproductive conditions. Within the spectral seclusion imposed by the life sentence, gardening also allowed the prisoner to explore the *spirit* of certain key ideas—of regeneration and reconstruction, for example—in a reassuringly *gritty*, material medium.

It is telling, though probably coincidental, that two major southern African novels of the period, Bessie Head's *A Question of Power* (1974), and J. M. Coetzee's *Life and Times of Michael K* (1983), find in the activity of gardening a potent symbol of endurance and new life. In a country divided by conflict, the distraction of gardening could of course represent a questionable refusal of politics, yet it equally signified a position from which to proceed beyond conflict, to reshape the world, even if in a small way.

In *A Question of Power*, the "full-time work" of a communal garden project represents psychological healing after a punishing period of madness. In cataloging, seeding, planting, watering—in gooseberries, tomatoes, cauliflower—Elizabeth the protagonist discovers a confirmation of the ordinary that opens her heart to a feeling of unity with humankind. Coetzee's K, a vagrant "Gardener, Grade 1," on the run from a series of institutions and camps, explores through the "exultant" cultivation of his pumpkins, squashes, and melons a means of transitory survival, an important source of continuity between the past and the present, the earth and animal life. For him it is also, significantly, a way of evading the camps that threaten to fence him round.

With his cultivation of a patch of earth—discovering a common love of soil and plant-rearing with his captors—Mandela developed important insights into the qualities of forbearance and cooperation, and into the *accommodations* that eventual mastery, including self-mastery, would entail. He commented:

> In prison, a garden is one of the few things you can really master and call your own. . . . The feeling of being the steward of this tiny patch of earth is a small taste of freedom.

As well as supplying a life-affirming sanctuary away from, if enclosed by, the morbid prison world, husbanding a garden could, in other words, assume certain of the aspects of creating a self-sufficient community or *fostering a nation*—as well as remaking a self. Coaxing life out of the earth, Mandela saw that mere ruthlessness would prove inimical to national unity:

law would always be more constructive than war. In a 1976 letter, he suggestively used an image of a growing plant as a symbol for political work.

At an interpersonal level, too, gardening provided a space where common interests between prisoner and warder could be plotted, and Mandela's early conviction that "all men have a core of decency" explored. It is probably true to say that gardening, this one opportunity for "free," constructive activity, became the primary dimension through which Mandela perceived that the mutual recognition of *humanness*—the regenerative concept of *ubuntu*—was fundamental to national transformation. Taking these different perspectives together, we see how it was in prison that he moved decisively away from thinking in terms of received ideas of the political struggle as a racially polarized conflict.

If we accept that Mandela's gardening contributed to how he set about forging a new political understanding for South Africa, we discern in the process an example of how he transformed his *practice into* a *theory* of national reconciliation, something that must count among his primary achievements. Just as he worked to convert the island's "culture of dialogue" (Soyinka's phrase) into a strategy of negotiation, the work of practical husbandry, too, translated into the painstaking vigilance with which he approached his government interlocutors, introducing his views to them, keeping them talking, yet consulting with the ANC.

The historian Antoinette Burton's work on the relation of the domestic space to the unfolding of public history suggests that the enclosed structure of an individual's living environment determines their understanding of both family and national life. Her theory pertains to Indian women in particular, yet it can be applied to how a long-term political prisoner like Mandela interacted with national history from his spartan cell: to how he derived protocols for action from working the confined yet adaptive and creative spaces of his garden plots.

Mac Maharaj once summarized his leader's style of debate as "proceeding from *their* assumptions and carefully marshalling arguments to move them to his conclusions. His line of advance [was] developed on the other party's line of attack": it was an intensely strategic, and spatialized, approach. As this suggests, shut away together with a group of trusted interlocutors committed to one-to-one dialogue, Mandela's situation molded his eventual rules of engagement with the Afrikaner government. It shaped the parameters—accommodating, other-directed, determined and secretive but open-ended—within which he set about mapping the road to a national peace.

As with his prison cell, so too with his gardens. His cultivation projects read Mandela a lesson in proceeding with caution, yet productively also. The man who once, as a political leader on the run, had no home life to speak of and certainly no time for a garden, now learned to appreciate the value of slowness, tactility, and proximity, of incremental change and the simple bonds of human cooperation. In this there is a partial analogy with how Gandhi used the feminine task of spinning *khadi* yarn to articulate his politics. In Mandela's case, however, his gardening did not represent a public performance, developed political stance, or gender declaration. The position of pragmatic reformism he arrived at via his gardening and prison dialogues was learned intuitively, day to day, and on the job, without ostentation. Moreover, given that this confined space, his long-term "home," was not in fact homely or welcoming, he developed a particularly intimate, even proprietorial, relationship to his wider national home, South Africa, to the extent of acting unilaterally once the time came to rescue that home from civil war.

· · · · ·

Go end there
One fine day
Where never till then
Till as much as to say
No matter where
No matter when

*Samuel Beckett, "Brief Dream," in* For Nelson Mandela *(1986)*

· · · · ·

# EIGHT

## Mandela's Ethical Legacy

●

IN LEWIS NKOSI'S 2006 *BILDUNGSROMAN*, *Mandela's Ego*, the Zulu boy Dumisa grows up with the sense of Mandela as his life-mentor and second father—the invisible household spirit shaping the different stages of his life. Most South Africans could be described in the same terms as Dumisa. Mandela is the myth that they have lived and in some cases died by. His legacy extends everywhere through their lives, as a kind of pervasive music, yet the populous twenty-first-century country must at the same time look to a future beyond their Madiba. In journalist Sandile Dikeni's words: "My people are this many and more and their collective name is bigger than that of Nelson Mandela."

Outside the Houses of Parliament in Cape Town where Nelson Mandela once presided, a street trader has a stall under the historic oak trees.

**On the historic election day of April 27, 1994,** Mandela cast his ballot at Ohlange High School in Inanda, South Africa—located, symbolically, in the heart of Zululand, the seat of the Inkatha Freedom Party.

He is among tens of other street traders here in the one-time Dutch East India Company garden. A short way off, as the ironies of historical proximity have it, stands a statue of the imperialist Cecil John Rhodes pointing north into Africa, at its base the words, "Behold Your Hinterland." The trader says he is proud of his wares. No, these are not batik items, he explains, but cloth cured in varying densities of rooibos tea. The subject of these painted cloths, none affordable to locals, is African wildlife. The only human subject is Nelson Mandela, full-face, hopeful, staring out into South Africa along the sight lines marked by Rhodes.

In 1994 Nelson Mandela and his Government of National Unity founded the new South African republic on the basis of social justice, racial reconciliation, and a revised postcolonial humanism. "The sun shall never set on so glorious a human achievement," Mandela optimistically ended his May 10 inaugural address. Yet, as his passionate urgings at the time betrayed, even though his struggle credentials allowed him to appeal directly to his people, his ethical republic was built on a fragile foundation. Most South African citizens were entirely unused to working within democratic structures, and the economy remained largely unreconstructed, with whites continuing to control the bulk of the country's capital.

Nearly a decade on from when Mandela stood down as first democratic president, it remains difficult to encapsulate his legacy. This is due in great part to his multifarious achievements, but in part, too, to the new South African state's mixed record on addressing the desperate inequalities of the past. It is also a consequence of the fact that, though lauded as a standard-bearer for *ethical leadership*, a moral colossus, and beacon of probity in a dark time, Mandela has simultaneously been, as we have seen, a *consummate performer*. It has been his particular talent to appear to different audiences in a range of convincing guises.

Throughout his presidency, Mandela in many ways remained the city showman, for whom it was not sufficient to be charming to all, but also to be recognized and even praised as such. A post-1994 example of his change-ability was that he advised his administration to seek an ethical foreign policy, yet condoned the sale of South African-made armaments to countries like Algeria and Colombia whose human rights records were poor, yet whose leaders had been ANC sympathizers. Earlier on, too, while in prison, according to James Sanders's *Apartheid's Friends*, Mandela apparently took different views on his then-wife's support for necklacing depending on whom he was addressing. How will the future assess Madiba, given these inconsistencies? Awkward though it may be to speculate without much benefit of hindsight, in what ways might this charismatic, yet sometimes Machiavellian character be regarded fifty or one hundred years from today?

Even with the new millennium well under way, there is no doubt that the reputation Mandela achieved at the end of the last century as a warrior for freedom and founder of a new democratic state remains assured. Yet the custodians of his reputation continue to be hard at work consolidating his legacy via all manner of hagiographical material, like coffee table "portraits" and children's storybooks, and through his different charities and foundations. These efforts to gild his already shining name suggest that his historical contribution may not be invulnerable to critique. Potentially he has powerful detractors, both radical and right-wing, though at present they hold fire out of respect for the Old Man's great age.

· · · · ·

"If there is any significant role that I played, it was that of being a vessel through which the struggle was presented to the nation and the world. The struggle had to have a symbol for it to be effective. The great men and women of the struggle chose that I be that symbol. If this was a good thing, praise must go to those who made the choice."

*Nelson Mandela, interview with Oprah Winfrey (April 2001)*

• • • • •

Mandela was a leader who strove to be all things to all people: this is one area that could be susceptible to critical reassessment. He was an African nationalist among African nationalists, a socialist in relation to his SACP colleagues, a South African patriot when in dialogue with Afrikaners. He was the electioneering president-in-waiting who in 1994 denied the emerging HIV/AIDS epidemic in South Africa so as not to lose votes for the already massively popular ANC. For P. W. Botha, he was the African gentleman who knew about Afrikaner history. For Fidel Castro, in virtually the same period, he remained a stalwart revolutionary and loyal comrade-in-arms. He was who his audience wanted him to be, a reflection of their best aspirations.

At certain points, however, when he deemed it historically expedient, he was not afraid to impose his vision, whether on supporters or opponents. This combination of *malleability* with the occasional authoritarian impulse, or of broad receptivity with a sporadically uncompromising *individualist will*, was determined in some measure by his overriding concern to achieve social harmony. He sought not to ignore differences so much as to set up moral codes that could be more or less agreed by all. On matters of common interest (armed struggle, negotiation, reconciliation), he could speak clearly and directly to his people. Yet in some situations his consensus-building meant that he controversially took pains to view a conflict from the point of view of *the other*, as well as of his own party.

It remains clear that we must seek the lasting legacy of Mandela's long struggle for freedom in the domain of the ethical and not the economic, the figural and not the material. He stood for a great cause, the fight against apartheid. He responded to his country's desperate need for redemption and strong tradition of millennial myths by presenting himself as a savior-figure. Nationally and internationally, he is perceived as an ethical giant towering over the twentieth century. More practically, he proved across his life a farsighted strategist for political freedom and a powerful activist-intellectual distinguished by fine moral intuitions. He never ceased to wrestle with, revise, and reclarify his political claims, all the while remaining aware of South Africa's need for the liberatory myth that he himself embodied. If Ghassan Hage is right in suggesting that a nation offers its citizens a sense of entitlement in that it allows them hope for the future, then among Mandela's key achievements is to have outlined new possibilities of hope for all South African citizens, both fearful whites and deprived nonwhites.

But he has also been an *architect of compromise*—almost necessarily so. In that respect, his ongoing road to freedom has in certain areas been end-stopped. He did not insist upon the socialist state that the 1955 Freedom Charter proclaimed and he still claimed to espouse in the early 1990s. He did not choose to found his country's new political equalities on the basis of social and economic policies that would firmly erase entrenched patterns of uneven development. Today's South Africa remains crisscrossed by margins and exclusive zones, though in foreign policy it has played a successful role as a broker of multilateral initiatives. As Neville Alexander observes, the negotiated settlement Mandela presided over precluded the realization of some of the most modest electoral promises of reconstruction. The question of course is: could Mandela or his government ever have honored such promises? The abolition of apartheid represented a hugely ambitious project, involving thoroughgoing regime change at every level. In the context of the Cold War's end, some might contend, the success of South Africa's democratic experiment required a Faustian pact of adjustment to the neoliberal world system. Which is to say, as Hage too admits, new hope works well with capitalism.

• • • • •

"I have walked that long road to freedom. I have tried not to falter; I have made missteps along the way. But I have discovered the secret that after climbing a great hill, one only finds that there are many more hills to climb. I have taken a moment here to rest, to steal a view of the glorious vista that surrounds me, to look back on the distance I have come. But I can rest only for a moment, for with freedom come responsibilities, and I dare not linger, for my long walk is not yet ended."

*Nelson Mandela, final paragraph,* Long Walk to Freedom *(1995)*

• • • • •

## Humanist Vision

At crucial points across his career, Mandela set himself up as the figure of the selfsame political and ethical positions that he was working to achieve: justice, nonracialism, social understanding. In his speeches he used his own experiences to illustrate his politics, and both before and after his incarceration was not averse to molding his political image in order to fit in with his media representations, when this was helpful to his cause. His party corroborated this process by establishing, as the centerpiece of its ideological self-legitimation, the myth of Madiba as redemptive national leader. For his countrymen, he became an *imaginative force field* in which a variety of different constituencies could invest meaning. In several recent South African novels, Ndebele's *The Cry of Winnie Mandela*, Dangor's *Bitter Fruit* (both 2003), as well as *Mandela's Ego* (2006), Mandela stalks through now as intimidating legend, now as benign figure of authority.

As this book demonstrates, *Mandela the life* courts a metaphorical reading. In particular, I suggest, the life asks to be read critically as a postcolonial practice: that is, as a theory of political resistance and social transformation *in action*; as the assertion of a *new humanism*. If colonialism involves separating human beings from their inclinations, then a postcolonial response is to restore people to a sense of self-belief. As several commentators observe, Mandela over the years found a way of converting his respect for the human dignity in each and every person into a political practice through dialogue: making cross-border conversation a culture-wide expectation, and a means of mapping common ground and mutual regard. For him, national reconciliation involved convincing South African citizens by example to act on the same respect. What, then, are the central insights that his *lived theory of transformation* offers?

With the end of apartheid, it was often said, South Africans could begin to appreciate the ordinary in life: in work, play, romance. The influential critic of the *rediscovered ordinary* Njabulo Ndebele explained that, in contrast with apartheid, which with its excesses of violence was nothing but spectacular, in a postapartheid world the normal life that people had struggled to maintain could now be recognized in all its nuance and complexity. By a process of logical conflation, in so far as he was perceived as a creator of the new South Africa, could Mandela with his fondness for dialogue, sensitivity to ambivalence, and sense of humor plausibly be viewed as a champion of the ordinary?

Attractive as the description might be, the answer to this question is: probably not. Despite his preference for living a simple life, Mandela

· · · · ·

"[Even that] old man with the smile of a mischievous child, Madiba, whom he once thought of as the saving grace of the older world: they all have the same brittle air of vulnerability, of souls fallow despite years of feverish cultivation. 'The struggle' sowed the seeds of bright hopes and burning ideals, but look at what they are harvesting: an ordinariness, but also a vanity fed by sly and self-seductive glimpses in the mirrors of their personal histories."

*Achmat Dangor, from* Bitter Fruit *(2003)*

· · · · ·

is of course not by any stretch ordinary, neither as human being nor as cultural phenomenon. Across his life, as Sophiatown speechmaker and underground guerrilla, he mounted spectacles of defiant justice that in terms of impact equaled the perverse spectacles of apartheid. If anything, his claim to being like you and me reinforced their magnitude by sly contrast. So it cannot be *merely* in the concept of a recuperated day-to-day that his symbolic achievement is centered.

Completing a development that began with his turn to multiracialism circa 1950, Mandela in jail began to shift the ground of his concept of human identity from the partial and racialized, to something more universal and reciprocal. Moving through diverse situations of one-to-one interaction, Mandela increasingly approached others not as members of a certain party or group, but as human beings first and foremost, as unpredictable, complicated, yet always ethical (or potentially ethical) agents. He became more interested in likeness than in difference; he focused on interaction, not distinction or separation.

In relation to postcolonial thought in Africa, which has conventionally focused on the polarized conflict of oppressor and oppressed, Mandela restored the idea of the fellow human being—the human perceived not as fixity, but as fluid, multifarious, poetic, and, most importantly, defined through reciprocity. His political vision grew out of anticolonial, antiapartheid practice, yet it developed through his prison dialogues and the negotiations with his enemy into a hope for involvement that defied antimony.

Although Mandela has never disregarded the risk and uncertainty that accompanies the process of approaching the other, his expanded understanding of the fellow human being coordinates to an extent with the Christianized humanist concept of *ubuntu* popularized by Desmond Tutu. This is reflected in Tutu's Nguni saying *umntu ngumntu ngabantu*, which means, "a person is a person through other people," or "my selfhood is contingent upon your selfhood": *I am well if you are well.* In Mandela's case, the thought translates into his 1985 speech refusing Botha's conditional release, when he tells his people, "Your freedom and mine cannot be separated." Such a reciprocal recognition of contingency, an adventurous openness to the other's humanness, was self-evidently anathema to the apartheid system.

Toward the end of Fanon's canonical call to arms *The Wretched of the Earth*, he looks forward to the day when the new postcolonial nation will produce "new men." His conclusion speaks urgently of how the Third World is to rehumanize the masses of humankind and rewrite history, but not by imitating Europe, which always proceeds by way of deadly oppositions. Instead, by making new, intensified connections, the Third World will create a humanity that exceeds and cancels the colonial experience.

By way of his tentative dialogic practices both in prison and beyond, Mandela contributed forcefully to the postcolonial redefinition of the human proclaimed by Fanon, yet at the same time pulled it in a different direction. To the new humanism he added, first, the idea that the colonized remake themselves through forms and energies *other than*—or at least in addition to—those involved in death. That is to say, he disposed of Fanon's "irrepressible violence" as a means of making history, and instead championed conversation, trust, and listening.

His second key contribution to the tantalizing definition of a reshaped, more inclusive humanism was subtly but determinedly to Africanize it (as in *ubuntu*). Always reminding supporters and enemies alike of his African-ness, he brought his humanism in line with the values of social harmony and mutual support that had always lain at the heart of African socialism. As the pan-nationalist Aimé Césaire might have said, his was a humanism made to the measure *both* of the world *and* of Africa, defined from the perspective of those whose humanity had historically been denied. Radically, the African was at the center of his concept of the human, and *not* the margin or outside against which the human was understood, as was more conventional.

The ideals of the Enlightenment, humanity and freedom, were notoriously defined in contradistinction to Africa, haunted by the figure of the racialized black "other." In consequence, it became impossible to think of an African identity, modern or traditional, not predicated upon the prejudicial constructions of Western reason. Mandela's enactment of a revised, open humanism effectively responded to these two colonial conundrums. Even as he articulated the reasoning of the law and the state, in court as in government, he at the same time performed these specifically and self-consciously as a black man, a black African.

Throughout, Mandela's refusal of a rigidly coherent doctrine gave him the opportunity to make challenging juxtapositions, such as of African-ness and rationality. As in his delicately balanced building of consensus, he interleaved aspects of African tradition with colonial modernity by casting these as already modern, yet as unique and native. African identity, he said in 1997, had always been "the product of our engagement in world history." His self-presentation in different public contexts decisively placed Africa within a range of categories—rationality, morality, justice—from which it had been excluded. His political methodology—learned, adept, full of wit—swept his continent in all its complexity into the narrative of world history.

*Nelson Mandela*—figure, icon, sign, smile—has been overrepresented to the point of being rendered banal, excavated for meaning till all sense of the human being behind the public face disappears. His story of overcoming is widely regarded as his country's ethical bequest to the new century. Yet, ironically, there is as yet no representation of Mandela that evokes possibly his greatest achievement, how he came to understand conversation as a human imperative. If there were such a representation, it would probably resemble improvised ensemble music, a complicated jazz rhythm scattering itself through time, impossible to recover exactly in script. A jazz riff alone would capture at once the risk and tenaciousness of Mandela's commitment to sheer talk: how he placed the idea of the human-in-interaction at the heart of his vision of the future.

**Nelson Mandela turned ninety years old** on July 18, 2008, and a number of tributes were held in his honor. Among them was a celebration held on August 2, 2008, at Loftus Versfeld Stadium in Pretoria; this photograph shows Mandela addressing the many well-wishers who had gathered at the event.

# FURTHER READING

•

**CHAPTER ONE**

On Mandela's life, the reliable biographies include:

Lodge, Tom. *Mandela: A Critical Life*. Oxford University Press, 2006.

Meer, Fatima. *Higher than Hope: The Authorized Biography of Nelson Mandela*. Hamish Hamilton, 1990 [1988].

Sampson, Anthony. *Mandela: The Authorized Biography*. HarperCollins, 2000.

On governing symbols:

Gordimer, Nadine. *Living in Hope and History*. Bloomsbury, 1990.

Hofmeyr, Isabel. *The Portable Bunyan: A Transnational History of The Pilgrim's Progress*. Princeton University Press, 2004.

Kalungu-Banda, Martin. *Leading like Madiba*. Double Storey, 2006.

Mangcu, Xolela, ed. *The Meaning of Mandela*. HCRC, 2006.

The complexities of life narrative:

Clifford, James. "Hanging Up Looking Glasses at Odd Corners: Ethnobiographical Prospects." In *Studies in Biography*, edited by D. Aaron. Harvard University Press, 1978.

Stanley, Liz. *The Autobiographical I*. Manchester University Press, 1992.

Cultural representation in Mandela's South Africa:

Coombs, Annie E. *History After Apartheid: Visual Culture and Public Memory in a Democratic South Africa*. University of the Witwatersrand Press, 2004.

De Kock, Leon, Louise Bethlehem, and Sonja Laden, eds. *South Africa in the Global Imaginary*. UNISA Press, 2004.

Layered postcolonial modernity:

Attwell, David. *Rewriting Modernity: Studies in Black South African Literary History*. University of KwaZulu-Natal Press, 2005.

Chakrabarty, Dipesh. *Provincializing Europe: Postcolonial Thought and Historical Difference*. Princeton University Press, 2000.

Mandela's idioms:

Cryws-Williams, Jennifer. *In the Words of Nelson Mandela*. Penguin, 1997.


**CHAPTER TWO**

On the iconography of national leaders:

Boehmer, Elleke. *Stories of Women: Gender and Narrative in the Postcolonial Nation*. Manchester University Press, 2005.

Cubitt, Geoffrey, and Allen Warren, eds. *Heroic Reputations and Exemplary Lives*. Manchester University Press, 2000.

Holden, Philip. *Autobiography and Decolonization*. Wisconsin University Press, 2006.

Colonial race pathologies:

DuBois, W. E. B. *The Souls of Black Folk*. Barnes and Noble, 2003.

Fanon, Frantz. *Black Skin, White Masks*. Translated by Charles Lam Markmann. Pluto, 1986 [1952].

Mandela—autobiographies/related memoirs:

Matthews, Frieda Bokwe. *Remembrances*. Mayibuye Books, 1995.

Kathrada, Ahmed. *Memoirs*. Zebra, 2004.

Mandela, Nelson. *Long Walk to Freedom*. Little, Brown, 1994.

Sisulu, Elinor. *Walter and Albertina Sisulu: In Our Lifetime*. Abacus, 2003.

Slovo, Gillian. *Every Secret Thing: My Family, My Country*. Little, Brown, 1997.

Further biographies:

Benson, Mary. *Nelson Mandela*. Rev. ed. Penguin, 1989.

Callinicos, Luli. *Oliver Tambo: Beyond the Engeli Mountains*. David Philip, 2004.

Guiloineau, Jean. *The Early Life of Rolihlahla Madiba Nelson Mandela*. Translated by Joseph Rowe. North Atlantic Books, 2002.

Meredith, Michael. *Nelson Mandela: A Biography*. Hamish Hamilton, 1997.

Nicol, Mike. "Narrative." In *Mandela: The Authorized Portrait*. Edited by Mac Maharaj, et al. PQ Blackwell, 2006.

Mandela's own words:

First, Ruth, ed. *No Easy Walk to Freedom*. Heinemann, 1965.

Quayson, Ato, ed. *No Easy Walk to Freedom*. Penguin, 2002.

International Defense and Aid Fund (ed.). *The Struggle Is My Life*. International Defense and Aid Fund, 1978.

Asmal, Kader, David Chidester, and Wilmot James, eds. *In His Own Words: From Freedom to the Future*. Abacus, 2004.

**CHAPTER THREE**

On apartheid and postapartheid:

Barber, James. *Mandela's World: The International Dimension*. James Currey, 1994.

Gumede, William M. *Thabo Mbeki and the Battle for the Soul of the ANC*. Zebra, 2005.

Harvey, Robert. *The Fall of Apartheid*. Macmillan, 2001.

Lodge, Tom. *Politics in South Africa from Mandela to Mbeki*. James Currey, 2003.

Meli, Francis. *South Africa Belongs to Us: A History of the ANC*. Zimbabwe Publishing House, 1988.

Sparks, Allister. *Tomorrow Is Another Country*. Heinemann, 1995.

Winnie Mandela:

Du Preez Bezdrob, Anné Mariè. *Winnie Mandela: A Life*. Zebra, 2003.

Gilbey, Emma. *The Lady: The Life and Times of Winnie Mandela*. Vintage, 1994.

Ndebele, Njabulo. *The Cry of Winnie Mandela: Novel*. David Philip, 2003.

Mandela's political analysis:

Mandela, Nelson. "Clear the Obstacles and Confront the Enemy" and "Whither the Black Consciousness Movement?" In *Reflections in Prison*. Edited by Mac Maharaj. Zebra, 2001.

Mandela, Nelson. "National Liberation." Unpublished essay, quoted in Anthony Sampson's *Mandela*.

**CHAPTER FOUR**

On African nationalism in transnational context:

Biko, Steve. *I Write What I Like*. Heinemann, 1978.

Gilroy, Paul. *The Black Atlantic: Modernity and Double Consciousness*. Verso, 1993.

Goebel, Walter, and Saskia Schabio, eds. *Beyond the Black Atlantic*. Routledge, 2006.

Johns, Sheridan, and R. Hunt Davis, Jr. *Mandela, Tambo, and the African National Congress: The Struggle against Apartheid 1948–1990*. Oxford University Press, 1991.

Padmore, George. *Pan-Africanism or Communism?* Dennis Dobson, 1956.

Cross-border collaboration:

Boehmer, Elleke. *Empire, the National, and the Postcolonial, 1880–1920.* Oxford University Press, 2002.

Gandhi, Leela. *Affective Communities: Anticolonial Thought, Fin-de-Siècle Radicalism, and the Politics of Friendship.* Duke University Press, 2006.

Young, Robert. *Postcolonialism.* Blackwell, 2001.

Gandhi in South Africa:

Bhana, Surendra. *Gandhi's Legacy: The Natal Indian Congress 1894–1994.* University of Natal Press, 1997.

Brown, Judith M., and Martin Prozesky, eds. *Gandhi and South Africa.* University of Natal Press, 1996.

Itzkin, Eric. *Gandhi's Johannesburg.* University of Witwatersrand Press, 2001.

Gandhi, M. K. *An Autobiography; or the Story of My Experiments with Truth.* Navajivan Publishing House, 1958 [1927].

Mandela, Nelson. "Gandhi the Prisoner." In *Mahatma Gandhi: 125 Years.* Edited by B. R. Nanda. Indian Council for Race Relations, 1995.

Mandela, Nelson. "The Sacred Warrior—Nelson Mandela on Gandhi." Time Magazine, January 3, 2000. http://www.time.com/time/time100/poc/magazine/the_sacred_warrior13a.html (accessed May 28, 2009).

Nehru:

Nehru, Jawaharlal. "From Lucknow to Tripoli." In *The Unity of India: Collected Writings 1937–1940.* John Day, 1942.

Nehru, Jawaharlal. *An Autobiography.* Rev. ed. The Bodley Head, 1942.

Nehru, Jawaharlal. *The Discovery of India.* Oxford University Press, 2002.

Fanon:

Clayton, Anthony. *The Wars of French Decolonization.* Longman, 1994.

*Studies in a Dying Colonialism*, tr. Haakon Chevalier. Earthscan Press, 1989.

Fanon, Frantz. *The Wretched of the Earth.* Translated by Constance Farrington. Penguin, 1986 [1961].

**CHAPTER FIVE**

On Africa and modernity:

Comaroff, John and Jean. *Of Revelation and Revolution: Christianity, Colonialism, and Consciousness in South Africa.* University of Chicago Press, 1991.

Deutsch, J.-G., et al., eds. *African Modernities: Entangled Meanings in Current Debate.* James Currey, 2002.

The Sophiatown phenomenon:

Chapman, Michael, ed. *The Drum Decade: Stories from the 1950s.* 2nd ed. University of KwaZulu-Natal Press, 2001.

Coplan, David. *In Township Tonight!* Ravan Press, 1985.

Modisane, Bloke. *Blame Me on History.* Thames and Hudson, 1963.

Nixon, Rob. *Homelands, Harlem, and Hollywood.* Routledge, 1994.

Nkosi, Lewis. *Home and Exile.* Longman, 1965.

Sampson, Anthony. *Drum: The Making of a Magazine.* 3rd ed. Jonathan Ball, 2005.

Thema, Derreck. *Kortboy: A Sophiatown Legend.* Kwela Books, 1999.

Fictional/autobiographical reflections on Mandela:

Dangor, Achmat. *Bitter Fruit.* Atlantic Books, 2003.

Kuzwayo, Ellen. *Call Me Woman.* The Women's Press, 1985.

Mandela, Winnie, et al. *Part of My Soul Went with Him.* Norton, 1985.

Nkosi, Lewis. *Mandela's Ego.* Umusi, 2006.

Poetry about Mandela:

Bartlett, Richard, ed. *Halala Madiba: Nelson Mandela in Poetry.* Aflame Books, 2006.

Cronin, Jeremy. *Even the Dead.* Mayibuye Books, 1997.

Opland, Jeff. *The Dassie and the Hunter* (an account of Thembu praise-poet David Manisi). University of KwaZulu-Natal Press, 2005.

Soyinka, Wole. *Mandela's Earth.* Andre Deutsch, 1988.

**CHAPTER SIX**

Gender and nationalism:

Driver, Dorothy. "Drum Magazine 1951–9 and Gender." In *Text, Theory, Space.* Edited by Sarah Nuttall, et al. Routledge, 1993.

Nandy, Ashis. *The Intimate Enemy.* Oxford University Press, 1983.

Rajan, Rajeswari Sunder. *Real and Imagined Women.* Routledge, 1993.

Bodies under empire:

Collingham, E. M. *Imperial Bodies.* Polity, 2001.

Mbembe, Achille. "Faces of Freedom: Jewish and Black Experiences." *Interventions* 7, no. 3 (2005): 293–8.

Stoler, Ann Laura. *Carnal Knowledge and Imperial Power.* University of California Press, 2002.

Sylvester, Christine. "Bare Life as a Development/Postcolonial Problematic." *The Geographical Journal* 172, no. 1 (March 2006): 66–77.

Mandela's self-representation:

Derrida, Jacques, and Mustafa Tlili, eds. *For Nelson Mandela*. Translated by Franklin Philip, et al. Seaver Books, 1987 [1986].

Coetzee, J. M. "The 1995 World Cup." In *Stranger Shores*. Secker, 2001.

Kane, John. *The Politics of Moral Capital*. Cambridge University Press, 2001.

Salazar, Phillipe-Joseph. *An African Athens: Rhetoric and the Shaping of Democracy in South Africa*. Lawrence Erlbaum, 2002.

**CHAPTER SEVEN**

On embodying freedom and the future:

Cixous, Hélène. *Manna for the Mandelstams for the Mandelas*. Translated by Catherine McGillivray. Minnesota University Press, 1994.

Diala, Isidore. "Interrogating Mythology: The Mandela Myth and Black Empowerment." *Novel: A Forum on Fiction* 38, no. 1 (2004): 41–56.

Robben Island:

The Robben Island General Recreational Committee Archive 1966–91. UWC-Robben Island Mayibuye Archives. MCH 64: 50–82.

Alexander, Neville. *Robben Island Dossier 1964–74*. University of Cape Town Press, 1994.

Buntman, Fran Lisa. *Robben Island and Prisoner Resistance to Apartheid*. Cambridge University Press, 2003.

Daniels, Eddie. *There and Back: Robben Island 1964–1979*, 3rd edn. CTP Books, 2002.

Fugard, Athol, John Kani, and Winston Ntshona. "The Island." In *The Township Plays*. Edited by Dennis Walder. Oxford University Press, 1993.

Gregory, James. *Goodbye Bafana: Nelson Mandela, My Prisoner, My Friend*. Headline, 1995.

Maharaj, Mac. *Reflections in Prison*. Zebra, 2001.

Spectrality:

Derrida, Jacques. *Specters of Marx*. Translated by Peggy Kamuf. Routledge, 1994.

Derrida, Jacques. "Il faut toujours parler de L'Afrique du Sud au futur antérieur." *Newton Zebra* 11 (1998): 22–7.

Gardening as survival:

Coetzee, J. M. *Life and Times of Michael K*. Secker, 1983.

Harris, Verne, ed. *A Prisoner in the Garden: Opening Nelson Mandela's Prison Archive*. Nelson Mandela Foundation, 2004.

Head, Bessie. *A Question of Power*. Heinemann, 1973.
Spatial construction:

Barnard, Rita. *Apartheid and Beyond: South African Writers and the Politics of Place*. Oxford University Press, 2006.

Burton, Antoinette. *Dwelling in the Archive: Women Writing Home*. Oxford University Press, 2003.

**CHAPTER EIGHT**

On postcolonial South Africa:

Attridge, Derek, and Rosemary Jolly, eds. *Writing South Africa: Recent Literature and Its Challenges*. Cambridge University Press, 1998.

Dikeni, Sandile. *Soul Fire: Writing the Transition*. University of KwaZulu-Natal Press, 2002.

Nuttall, Sarah, and Cheryl-Ann Michael, eds. *Senses of Culture: South African Culture Studies*. Oxford University Press, 2000.

South Africa's neoliberalism:

Alexander, Neville. *An Ordinary Country: Issues in the Transition from Apartheid to Democracy in South Africa*. University of KwaZulu-Natal Press, 2002.

Bond, Patrick. *Elite Transition: From Apartheid to Neoliberalism in South Africa*. Pluto, 2000.

Marais, Hein. *South Africa, Limits to Change.* 2nd ed. Zed Books, 2001.

Nation, self, and other:

Appiah, Kwame Anthony. *Cosmopolitanism: Ethics in a World of Strangers*. Allen Lane, 2006.

Derrida, Jacques, and Anne Dufourmantelle. *Of Hospitality.* Translated by R. Bowlby. Stanford University Press, 2000.

Gikandi, Simon. "Race and the Idea of the Aesthetic." *Michigan Quarterly Review* 40, no. 2 (Spring 2001): 318–50.

Hage, Ghassan. *Against Paranoid Nationalism*. Pluto, 2003.

Mandela for children:

*Madiba Magic: Nelson Mandela's Favorite Stories*. Tafelberg, 2002.

# CHRONOLOGY

•

| | |
|---|---|
| **1846–7** | Frontier "War of the Axe" between British colonists in the eastern Cape, on the one hand, and the Xhosa and one branch of the Thembu people on the other. |
| **1857** | Cattle Killing movement in Transkei, led by prophetess Nongqawuse, leads to famine among the Xhosa people. |
| **1877–8** | Last Frontier War, in which migrant Thembu people support their neighbors, the Xhosa, and Transkei-based Thembu support the whites. |
| **1894** | Mohandas Gandhi founds Natal Indian Congress in Durban. |
| **1899–1902** | Anglo-Boer War. |
| **1906** | Bambata Zulu rebellion, sparked by refusal to pay poll tax. |
| **1910** | Union of South Africa. |
| **1912** | Formation of South African Native National Congress (from 1923, the ANC). |
| **1913** | Native Land Act: 87% of South Africa's land officially allocated to whites. |
| **1918** | End of World War I. |
| | July 18: Nelson Mandela born in Mvezo, Transkei. |
| **1920** | Black miners' strike quashed. |
| | Mandela moves with his mother and sisters to Qunu following his headman father's dismissal by a white magistrate. |
| **1923** | South African Indian Congress formed. |
| **1925** | Mandela starts school and is given European name by teacher Miss Mdingane. |
| **1926** | Balfour Declaration. |
| **1927** | Legislation against interracial sexual relations. |
| | Following his father's death, Mandela goes to live with guardian, Chief Jongintaba. |
| **1931** | December: first pass-burning demonstrations. |
| **1933** | Coalition of Afrikaner parties under Hertzog and Smuts (collapses in 1939 with country's decision to go to war). |

| 1934 | Mandela circumcised along with his cousin Justice. |
|------|---|
| 1935 | Mandela enrolls at Clarkebury Institute mission school. |
| 1936 | Native Land and Trust Act fixes 1913 land distribution in perpetuity. Africans lose Cape voting rights. |
| 1937 | Mandela attends Healdtown school. |
| 1939 | World War II begins. |
| | Mandela enrolls at Fort Hare University to train as a civil servant. |
| 1940 | Hertzog and Malan launch reformed National Party. |
| | Mandela leaves Fort Hare without completing his degree after association with SRC strike. |
| 1941 | Mandela and Justice flee arranged marriages by running away to Johannesburg. Through businessman Walter Sisulu, Mandela finds a position as clerk with legal firm of Witken, Sidelsky, and Eidelman, to complete a degree by correspondence, graduating in 1942. |
| 1942 | Mandela joins ANC. |
| 1943 | Enrolls for LLB degree at Johannesburg's Witwatersrand University. August: successful Alexandra bus boycott. |
| | Formation and (in 1944) launch of ANC Youth League with Sisulu (Treasurer), Oliver Tambo (Secretary), and Mandela as executive member. |
| 1944 | Marries first wife, Evelyn Mase. Completes legal articles and begins full-time study. |
| 1945 | Son Madiba Thembekile (Thembi) born. |
| 1946 | African mine workers' strike. |
| 1947 | Mandela elected to Transvaal provincial ANC executive and opposes SACP-SAIC-ANC "Votes for All" campaign. |
| 1948 | Afrikaner Nationalist Party under Daniel Malan wins power with the explicit agenda of bringing racial segregation (apartheid) into law. |
| | First daughter, Makaziwe, born, who dies at nine months. |
| 1949 | December: ANCYL gains control of ANC executive. |
| 1950 | Raft of new Acts—Population Registration, Group Areas, Suppression of Communism—hammers the white sepulcher of apartheid into place. |
| | ANCYL permits new multiracial policy. |
| | Mandela joins ANC national executive. |
| | June 26: helps organize ANC-SAIC "Day of Mourning." |
| | September: elected ANCYL president. |
| | Second son, Makgatho, born. |
| 1952 | ANC-SAIC Defiance Campaign. |
| | Mandela placed under banning order. Passes attorney's professional examinations and opens legal office at Chancellor House, Johannesburg, with Tambo. |

|      | Elected President of Transvaal Provincial ANC, then ANC Deputy President. Albert Luthuli elected ANC President. |
|------|---|
| **1953** | Bantu Education Act. Mandela resigns from ANC to accommodate banning order. |
| **1954** | Sophiatown evictions. |
|      | Daughter Pumla Makaziwe (Maki) born. |
| **1955** | June 26: Congress of the People at Kliptown, Johannesburg. Freedom Charter (foundation of future South African constitution) adopted. |
|      | ANC's Bantu Education boycott fails. |
| **1956** | August 9: Women's March on Pretoria to protest against pass laws. Bus boycotts across Johannesburg. |
|      | December 6: 156 men and women representing ANC, SAIC, Colored People's Congress, and Congress of Democrats arrested and charged with high treason. Treason Trial begins ( –1961). |
| **1957** | Marriage to Evelyn breaks down. |
| **1958** | Mandela marries second wife, Nomzamo Winifred Madizikela (Winnie), a social worker. |
| **1959** | Pan-African Congress splits from ANC. |
|      | International Anti-Apartheid Movement launched. |
|      | Daughter Zenani born. |
| **1960** | March 21: Sharpeville massacre of sixty-nine black protestors under police fire. State of emergency declared: Twenty thousand arrested, two thousand detained without trial. ANC and PAC banned. |
|      | Daughter Zindziswa born. |
| **1961** | March: Treason Trial accused found not guilty. Mandela disappears underground. |
|      | South Africa, declared a republic, leaves the Commonwealth. |
|      | December: launch of Umkhonto we Sizwe. |
| **1962** | Mandela travels in Africa and Europe: receives military training, meets leading activists and politicians. August 5: he is captured in Kwa-Zulu-Natal Midlands and sentenced to five years' imprisonment. |
| **1963** | Ninety-Day Detention Act. Mandela sent to Robben Island, recalled after Liliesleaf Farm raid, Rivonia. Charged with sabotage and planning an armed invasion. Rivonia Trial begins. |
| **1964** | April 20: Mandela delivers statement from dock. |
|      | June 12: Eight Rivonia Trialists sentenced to life imprisonment. |
| **1968** | Steve Biko forms South African Students' Organization. Mandela's mother dies. |
| **1969** | May: Winnie Mandela detained under Terrorism Act for 491 days. |
|      | July: Thembi dies in a car crash. Mandela not permitted to attend his funeral. |

| 1974–5 | Fall of Salazar's Portugal leads to independence of Angola and Mozambique. |
|---|---|
| | Mandela writes secret autobiography. |
| 1976 | Internal Security Act. |
| | South African invasion of Angola. |
| | June 16: Soweto students' uprising against Bantu Education leaves 618 dead, fifteen hundred wounded, over thirteen thousand arrested. |
| | Mandela refuses offer of conditional reduction of sentence. |
| 1977 | May 17: Winnie Mandela placed under banning order in Brandfort. |
| | September 12: Biko killed in detention and BC organizations banned. |
| 1979 | Mandela awarded Nehru Prize for International Understanding in absentia. |
| 1980 | Launch of worldwide AAM Release Mandela campaign. |
| | June 1: ANC Special Operations bombs SASOL oil refinery. |
| 1982 | Mandela and four other Rivonia prisoners moved to Pollsmoor Prison. |
| 1983 | Formation of UDF, embracing non-banned anti-apartheid organizations. |
| 1984 | Nationwide resistance to new constitution enshrining population segregation. Nkomati Accord between South Africa and Mozambique. Bishop Desmond Tutu awarded Nobel Peace Prize. |
| 1985 | January 31: P. W. Botha offers Mandela conditional freedom. |
| | February 11: Mandela responds with Soweto speech read by daughter Zindzi: a prisoner, like an unfree people, "cannot give undertakings on violence." |
| | Congress of South African Trade Unions formed. Resistance to apartheid builds across a broad front. |
| | July 20: State of emergency. |
| | December: Mandela has prostate operation and first meets Minister of Justice Kobie Coetzee. |
| 1986 | Mandela meets Commonwealth Eminent Persons Group. |
| | June 12: State of emergency renewed. |
| 1987 | November: first Rivonia prisoner Govan Mbeki released, due to ill health. |
| 1988 | February: UDF banned. |
| | March: South African defeat at Cuito Cuanavale. |
| | July: Free Mandela Campaign organizes seventieth birthday celebrations at Wembley Stadium, London. |
| | December: Mandela transferred to Victor Verster after tuberculosis treatment. |
| 1989 | F. W. de Klerk takes over from Botha as state president. |
| 1990 | February 11: Mandela walks free. |
| | April: "talks about talks" between government and ANC. |

|      | August: ANC renounces use of arms. |
| **1991** | Mandela elected ANC president. |
|      | December: Convention for a Democratic South Africa. |
| **1992** | White referendum shows pro-reform majority. |
|      | Formal separation from Winnie. |
| **1993** | Assassination of SACP leader Chris Hani. |
|      | September: creation of transition executive council. |
|      | October: Mandela and de Klerk jointly receive Nobel Peace Prize. |
|      | November 18: Adoption of new constitution. |
| **1994** | April 27–28: nineteen million South Africans participate in first democratic elections. |
|      | May 10: Mandela inaugurated as president. |
| **1995** | Mandela awarded Order of Merit by Queen Elizabeth II. |
|      | November: Nigerian writer-activist Ken Saro-Wiwa executed despite Mandela's diplomacy. |
| **1996** | April: Truth and Reconciliation Commission, modeled on Chile's 1990 Comisión, chaired by Archbishop Tutu, begins two years of hearing testimonies from apartheid's victims. |
|      | Divorce from Winnie. |
| **1998** | Mandela marries Graça Machel. |
| **1999** | South Africa has highest number per capita of people living with HIV/AIDS in the world (four–five million = 10% of population). |
|      | June: ANC wins second general election. Mandela hands over to Thabo Mbeki. |
| **2000** | Mandela formally retires from public life. |
| **2002** | Formally promotes HIV/AIDS awareness. |
| **2005** | Announces son Makgatho's death from AIDS. |
| **2006** | Awarded Amnesty's Ambassador of Conscience award. |
| **2007** | Statue of Mandela unveiled in Westminster Square, London. |

# INDEX

•

Note: Page numbers in *italics* include illustrations and photographs/captions.

# PICTURE CREDITS

•